# A THERAPY FOR DYING DEMOCRACIES

by Theodore C. Stathis

Dorrance Publishing Co
585 Alpha Drive
Pittsburgh, PA 15238
Visit our website at *www.dorrancebookstore.com*

ISBN: 978-1-6386-7044-5
eSIBN: 978-1-6386-7992-9

# About the Author

**Theodore C. Stathis** has the equivalent of a B.Sc. degree from the Technical University in Vienna, as well as a M.Sc. and an Eng. Sc.D. degree from Columbia University, New York.

He is President of the Foundation for Mediterranean Studies.

He has worked as an Assistant Researcher at Columbia University, New York, and as an Assistant Professor at Manhattan College, New York, and at New York University, where he also worked as a Researcher. He was a Scientific Expert, and later a lecturer, at the University of Patras, and a Visiting Professor at the University of Macedonia in Thessaloniki.

He was president of Advanced Acoustic Research Inc. in New York, Executive Director of N.B.G. Bancassurance, President and Executive Director of National Capital S.A. (National Bank of Greece Subsidiaries), and Adviser to the Board of the National Bank of Greece, as well as President of the Musical and Educational Organization of Greece (Athens Camerata – Friends of Music Orchestra).

He served for 15 years as a member of the Greek Parliament, and as an Undersecretary for the Greek Ministry of Defense, as a Deputy Minister for the Greek Ministry of Culture, and as Minister of Agriculture.

He is the composer of four operas (three of which have been performed at the Athens Concert Hall – MMA): *Antigone*, based on the play by Sophocles (see excerpts on YouTube), *Opus Elgin: the Destruction of the Parthenon*, *Alcestis* based on the play by Euripides, and *Theodora* (set in the time of Justinian); he has also composed a number of quartets for strings, and numerous songs.

As a writer, he has published several articles on science and politics, and he is the author of *National Defense and Its Achilles' heel*, *In Search of a Model for Democracy Today* and *The Trojan Horse of Democracy*.

# Personal Dedication

To my father, Christos, a democrat who over a period of nine months during the German occupation, gave refuge to a British fighter pilot, whose plane had been shot down by the Germans, hiding him in our house. On the authorities' wanted list for this "crime," he managed to escape the German collaborators, but was not as lucky when these same collaborators were now British collaborators. One night in November 1945, they stormed into the same house where the British fighter pilot had been hiding during the German occupation and butchered him before my eyes.

And, of course, to my mother, Joanna, who survived, despite receiving a serious knife wound on the back on that same tragic night, and who managed to make me what I am today.

# Contents

# Prologue

The motivation to write this book came from the 2010 Greek debt crisis. The idea of doing so was further strengthened when articles, as well as books, with titles such as "why or how democracies die," started appearing around the globe. As a reaction to these articles and books, some writers – primarily professors and specialists in the period of Classical Greece, when direct democracy was actively implemented, particularly in ancient Athens – began to remind people what direct democracy was about, also pointing out that what some writers presumed to be dying today has in fact little to do with real democracy. Their arguments were based mainly on the definition given to democracy by Aristotle, in his seminal work on the **Athenian *Politeia*,** the polis and constitution of his day. There, he specifically defines democracy as a system of government where the axiomatic principles of democracy were upheld and applied without exception, such as for example the precepts that all citizens are politically equal, that all are entitled to freedom of speech (provided that it does not restrict the corresponding freedom of speech of others), that there should be equal opportunities for all, that everyone should be equal before the law, and so on. Political equality in ancient Athens was ensured through the selection of all public officials (governors, members of parliament, and jurors) by **lot.** An electoral process was used only for the appointment of specialists, such as the ten generals. This process took place in the citizens' assembly, which was perceived as being incorruptible and free of ethical conflicts. The system of government whereby public officers were selected by election was labeled by Aristotle as **oligarchic** – that is, government by the few.

Modern "democracies" were the result of considerable popular pressure. At times, these social tensions have erupted into bloody uprisings against monarchs, oligarchs or dictators, especially during the last two or three centuries. Those in power have sought to reconcile these conflicts by way of an electoral process, aimed at "conceding" to people the right to vote. Some of these elections have been free, while others have been free in name only. The extent to which elections were truly free or not was determined by the different electoral laws. Yet regardless of the degree of freedom, and as has been shown elsewhere, the electoral process itself did not and does not ensure results that really represent the people's choices. There are many other factors – such as collusion, strong centers of influence that use every trick in the game, etc. – which contribute to the corruption of electoral results, and, ultimately, to the failure of elections to reflect real democracy. Such are, in effect, today's modern "democracies," over which so many tears are being shed daily by those who purport to be astonished by, and to be lamenting, their foretold death.

This leads naturally to the question of the remedy that should be applied to stop this process of demise. Some authors have written entire books that offer advice on how to rescue these regimes. Among them are also those who promote direct democracy in the way it was practiced in ancient Athens. The process seems to have worked there (albeit not always with good results). So why not make full use of it today? The ancient model could certainly work even better today with the help of technology, particularly if it were applied to small regions, as was the case for the city-state of ancient Athens. But when one seeks to apply this system unthinkingly, and without any changes or adjustments, to entire countries with significantly larger populations, then the process becomes unwieldy. There are many proponents of this theory today, which would, if used without any modifications, devolve into something far worse than the state of today's dying "democracies." What is required instead, is to use new legal and political instruments for the purpose of serving democracy far more effectively. The ancient Athenians' most important political instrument was the use of sortition (selection by lot) for the appointment of all public officials—a tool which ensured, in most cases, the normal, and collusion-free operation of direct democracy during the deliberations of the citizens' assembly. The use of this tool by the Athenians resulted in the active presence in the citizens' assembly of all 500 members of parliament, and of many of the six thousand sworn jurists. Furthermore, any male citizen over the age of twenty could also participate in the citizens' assembly.

Based on my twenty years of experience as a parliamentarian and as a cabinet minister, what I hope to accomplish is to identify ways of using this political instrument in order to ensure at every level of political decision-making the presence of voters who may be free of all outside controlling influence, and of public officials who are selected through the electoral process; also, to do so from the outset without a concurrent necessity for radical reforms which could result in chaos. What is more, the kind of reforms I will be proposing here may inspire a true revival of today's declining democracies, and lead to their transformation into better democracies. In order for this change to take place, what is required is only the will of the people, and nothing else; more importantly, this critical change does not require any prior constitutional changes, such as the ones which would be the precondition for the implementation of the model of a citizens' assembly.

In closing, I would like to thank Peri Pamir, a political scientist, for reading the manuscript and for providing very helpful suggestions, Dr. Rainer Boehmer for checking the preliminary version of this work, and Mika Provata-Carlone for editing the final version of the manuscript.

Theodore C. Stathis

# Chapter One

## 1.1 On Democracy

The aim of this chapter is to introduce the reader to the history and to some basic concepts of democracy as a political system of government. It was initially invented by the ancient Athenians and was subsequently also used by city-states in other parts of Greece. Democracy was born at around 508 B.C., and it has gone through substantial changes since that time, to such an extent that the forms it assumes today bear little connection to real democracy. They may use in their constitutional declarations the axiomatic principles of democracy as the basis of their ideology, but in practice these are not upheld. Aristotle, in fact, describes them as oligarchic systems of government. In our times, they have been transformed, at best, into such oligarchic systems because of the use of the political instrument of electoral voting for the selection of politicians. In ancient Athenian democracy voting was never used to select politicians. It was used during the deliberations of the citizens' assembly for the election of specialists, and during votes on decrees or laws, or in order to arrive at a judgement on specific sentences; it was used in parliament on similar occasions, and in the courts of justice for the purpose of deciding on a sentence. These bodies were perceived as being immune to collusion, which is why voting was used in their case.

Before the invention of democracy, city-states, or any other unified group of people, had different systems of government, which were generally quite repressive.

The institution of democracy serves states which care about the welfare of their people. However, democracy can also serve all kinds of human associations.

It is clear that in any organized social group the interests of the various individuals will differ widely, as no two people are identical. This diversity is actually what makes the world move forward. Let us then further assume that people in general would want to belong to a union, and even support it, as long as they could be sure that they would all benefit from it in the way prescribed by its constitution or its by-laws. This thesis seems to be supported by the data provided by the theory of the evolution of the species, and in particular by the process of evolution of *homo sapiens*. One sees all sorts of unions, which cover almost every aspect of human activity. In the political domain, such unions are the political parties. This reinforces, and in a way confirms, Aristotle's own observation: humans are not only social animals, they are also political ones.

Social and political unions may resolve certain problems for their members, but they can also create new ones. In all the different domains of human activity, it is such social and political unions that generally prevail. Unions are institutional structures which have been in most cases invented by their members. On certain occasions, however, an institutional structure may be common to more than one union with similar features. Democracy, for example, was invented by the ancient Greeks, but its axiomatic principles, and some of its tools, have been adopted by many other states, especially in our days. All institutional structures are designed for the purpose of serving one or more objectives of the union, and for this reason they are liable to changes when the objectives of the union are no longer being served. Institutional structures, therefore, cannot be equated with their objectives. They are ancillary to the objectives of a union.

Some institutional structures consist only of some method (or methods) through which it is assumed that the objectives of the union are being served. When it becomes clear that the method, or methods, no longer serve the objectives of the union, then these are changed, or should be changed. Such institutional structures are of a simple type. They do not contain any universal truths. There are, however, institutional structures which consist of a set of axiomatic principles expressing universal truths, and that also include a set of even simpler institutional structures. Such an institutional structure is the political system we call democracy, and its mission is the welfare of the people in their totality. Therefore, the institutional structure of democracy is not an end in itself; it is a tool for ensuring the welfare of all people living under its state. In such institutional structures, the initial axiomatic principles constitute the corner stones of the union, while the simpler institutional structures safeguard these foundations, in such a way as to ensure that the edifice erected on these cornerstone's remains firmly secure, even when it is threatened by severe earthquakes.

Democracy, as it first emerged in ancient Athens, was based on such a combination of principles and simple tools. It consisted of a set of axiomatic principles and of certain tools which operated according to particular rules. These "tools" were the parliament, the citizens' assembly, and the courts. This early version of democracy has been christened by some 'direct democracy,' because of the way decisions were being made by the institutional structure of the citizens' assembly. This latter enjoyed absolute power. All male citizens over the age of twenty had the right to participate in its sessions.

Some of the tools used in the system of ancient Athens, where it is thought that direct democracy was applied, will also be recommended for use in today's systems of government. However, they are going to be used in a slightly different manner, namely, as a basis upon which to build a proposed model that is specifically designed for today's democracies.

There is an extensive body of interesting literature about direct democracy in many languages. This present work references some of these books in the bibliography at the end. Of course, and as is the case with most things, direct democracy did not only have supporters, it also had very strong opponents. This is something that persists today. Some of these detractors are plain, ordinary people. Unfortunately, however, we equally have two other very strong forces of opposition, which represent specific models of production. One is the capitalist model of production, and the other is the Marxist model of production. One might also add a third one, which is man's intrinsic nature. A few observations on these questions will allow for a more comprehensive perspective regarding the advantages and disadvantages of direct democracy overall.

Direct democracy, as some call it, is a system of government invented by the ancient Greeks. Some first signs pointing towards a democratic system of government appeared during the seventh century B.C., yet concrete democratic initiatives were first undertaken around the beginning of the sixth century B.C. when **Solon,** as the leader of the Athenians, introduced a specific set of laws (597–596 B.C.). One of the laws that were passed during his time cancelled all the debt owed by poorer farmers to rich landowners, who treated these impoverished farmers almost like slaves. The center of government was principally the citizens' assembly, which had been devised by the aristocrats. In these assemblies only citizens of aristocratic descent could participate. One might say that this was in a way a restrictive democracy for the few, a system that Aristotle defines as oligarchic. Throughout the sixth century, no other major reforms were carried out until the very end of the period (508/7 B.C.), with **Cleisthenes**, the aristocratic leader of the democrats. Cleisthenes introduced, firstly, administrative reforms, aimed at consolidating the city-state of Athens by creating ten new sets of tribes, yet without abolishing the four that already existed (this was done by reorganizing the population); he also succeeded, secondly, through political reforms, in widening participation in government (a) through the use of sortition, that is, using a system of lots to select from among all male citizens over the age of 30 the holders of public office (parliamentarians), and also the sworn jurists who would serve in the people's jury-courts and (b) through broadening access to the citizens' assembly, by allowing all male citizens over the age of twenty to participate in its sessions, where they could also speak and vote. Each of the newly formed tribes consisted of an equal number of people of mixed geographic origin, a third of whom hailed from the city, another third from the villages of mainland Attica (the region where Athens is located), and one third from the villages along the seacoast. Before these reforms, the tribes had mostly been family clans fighting among themselves over-extending their areas of control. This reorganization brought to the surface the real struggle that lay beneath, namely the one between the rich and the poor. Sortition was used to select holders of public office from each of the so-called **trittyes** (where each **trittys** was a population division consisting of one third of each new type of tribe, like an electoral district). Sortition was also used to determine which three trittyes were to form the new sets of tribes.

This kind of administrative reorganization and consolidation of state structures was carried out during the same period elsewhere as well. One example was the Peloponnesian alliance, which was more sizeable than the city-state of Attica, to which Athens belonged; a far more extensive coalition was the Persian state under Darius I. However, in the city-state of Athens, democratic rule, using sortition, was a crucial feature. It is safe to say that consolidating the state structures did not in itself lead to democracy. It was rather the use of this important political tool, sortition, in the selection of public officials and sworn jurists, which was crucially conducive to the creation of this famous wonder called democracy.

Instead of sortition, today's "democracies" use the electoral process, either through general or local elections, for selecting the holders of public office, which is what people consider today as the democratic way to conduct politics. The ancient Greeks held the exact opposite view: elections were elitist and reserved for the nobility, more appropriate for oligarchic rule (the rule of the wealthy few) than for democracy, whereas sortition was the democratic way. The use of a system of lots ensured political equality among those members of society who were volunteering to serve the community (the new tribe), while the single term in office ensured in turn the presence of voters in assemblies such as the parliament or the jury courts, where voting took place for the passing of laws, for the approval of specialists, or for deciding on the sentencing or the acquittal of a citizen. These votes were free of any political dependency on leaders or on individual figures belonging to the same or any other tribe.

The electoral process constitutes the connecting bridge between candidates and voters, whoever they may be (poor or rich individuals, or larger centers of influence), and through which a dependency is created between the two parties involved, especially when renewal of a candidate's term in political office is at stake. It can imply the existence of bilateral favors between the candidate and certain "important" voters, who can make a difference as regards the electoral outcome. This dependency in turn thwarts the efforts to uphold the axiomatic principles of democracy, principles that one finds written in the constitutions of all Western democracies, and which ought to apply equally to all citizens.

At around 465 B.C., **Ephialtes**, another democratic leader, introduced a further important reform, whereby the leaders of all ten tribes, instead of being elected, would, from then on, be selected by lot (until then, only the members of parliament and members of the jury were selected by lot). At that time, all public officials worked unremunerated. Later, **Pericles** introduced a bill that provided salaries to all public officials, while ordinary citizens who did not hold any office were for the time being excluded from the scheme. Pericles' move was a political response to the actions of a rich Athenian named **Kimon**, the son of the famous **Miltiades,** who, as general, had led the Greek forces and defeated the Persian invaders of Greece. **Kimons' underhand dealings** involved, according to Pericles, the bribing of voters who participated in the deliberations of the citizens' assembly. The assembly was the governing body, and it enjoyed then absolute power. At around 392 B.C., the measure of salaries was extended to the members of the citizens' assembly as well, in order to boost citizen participation. Overall, all the leaders mentioned above played a part in setting the foundations for the "running" of direct democracy in ancient Athens, which also constituted the blueprint for some of the other city-states in Greece. In several of these city-states, and, most prominently, in Athens, this form of democracy was operational, with some interruptions, for a little over a century and a half (508–332 B.C.). It was during that period that the Parthenon was build, which has demonstrated ever since the level of expertise that the city-state of Athens had reached at that point in time in the various fields of human endeavor.

The political instruments of this system of government were the parliament, the jury courts, and the citizens' assembly (*Ecclesia*). The citizens' assembly was the political instrument by way of which all decisions were made or approved. It enjoyed absolute power, since it stood, in theory, for the institutional structure that gave power to the people. There was also a supreme court, which was charged with the duty of reassessing the decisions of the lower courts, but later, with the reforms introduced by Ephialtes, some of its jurisdictions were transferred to the citizens' assembly. Every male citizen over the age of twenty was free, and to a certain extent expected, to participate in the deliberations of the general assembly. This participation was not obligatory. Non-participating citizens were regarded as not adding value to society, yet there were many who could not participate in the assemblies, either because they were serving in the armed forces, or because they had to work for a living—and there were even others who were barred by law from attending. The average participation in the general assembly represented, at best, around 10% of the eligible voters, whose number ranged between 20,000 and 45,000, depending on the moment in time. The lower figure corresponds to periods of war.

**Parliament prepared the agenda for the upcoming discussions in the citizens' assembly, and in between sessions, it was responsible for overseeing the implementation of its decisions. This task was assigned to specialists, who were selected by vote during the assembly's sessions.** The members of parliament, 500 in total, were delegated by the ten tribes of the city-state (50 men from each tribe, also selected by lot). **The selection was made by sortition from among a pool of volunteers, and those who were thus chosen were required to serve for one year.** This procedure ensured that a very important axiomatic principle of democracy was invariably upheld, namely that of political equality among all citizens wishing to volunteer their services. The fact that sortition was only applied to a pool of volunteers, who had to serve, when the measure was first adopted, unremunerated, naturally resulted, during that period, in most parliamentarians coming from rich families, namely aristocratic. At first, this was not necessarily a negative factor, since the rich were also, most likely, educated.

During the entire course of ancient democracy, Greece successfully overcame many critical challenges, such as the Persian invasions; it developed impressive commercial activities with all the surrounding states and beyond, and the societies of each city-state acquired an exceptional level of knowledge and specialization in many trades and professions, in science and philosophy, and, of course, in the arts, history, rhetoric, poetry, and literature. At the start of the Renaissance, the combination of all these achievements would form the basis of modern Western civilization.

## 1.2 The Principles of Democracy

The principles of democracy, as proclaimed by its founders, were intended to be enjoyed by all Athenian citizens. However, the political instruments that were devised and used in order to serve these principles proved to be inadequate in practice. The principles of democracy were:

1. **It is the people who rule (Democracy > demos + kratos = the people + state power). This principle, in the way it was implemented, implied direct democracy.**
2. **Freedom of speech is every citizen's right, provided that their free speech does not restrict the free speech of the other members in that society.**
3. There is **political equality for all citizens. Namely, all citizens have the right to vote, and to be voted for public office (which does not carry political authority), if they meet the prerequisites for the post.**
4. There are **equal opportunities for everyone.**
5. All are **equal before the law (this applies to the poor as well as the rich).**

This set of principles would have also implied a set of responsibilities for each citizen of the city-state, both towards every other citizen and, of course, towards society. Those citizens who did not operate within these norms, were considered the enemies of democracy, and the consequences for them were very serious.

The main political instrument of power that was used to serve the above principles was the citizens' assembly. All male citizens over the age of twenty had the right to participate in its deliberations, where they could speak for an equal length of time as anyone else, and on any subject, vote on resolutions and laws, as well as on the election of specialists. Elections were held only in the citizens' assembly, and only in order to appoint specialists, such as the ten generals (one from each tribe); they were never used to elect politicians. Whether these principles were well served by the citizens' assembly remains to be examined later.

In ancient Athenian democracy all holders of public office were selected by sortition and for one term only. This method was chosen in order to observe the third principle, and to avert collusion. For the same reasons, all sworn jurists, six thousand in total, were also selected by sortition, and for a single term, in order to comply with the fifth principle, and also to emphasize the independence of the judiciary from the executive power, which was all vested in the citizens' assembly. It was also in the citizens' assembly that voting was held in order to confer Greek citizenship on foreigners who applied for it, or to impose certain types of punishment, such as the death sentence. The citizens' assembly, the sortition for selecting members of parliament and sworn jurists, and the single-term appointments of parliamentarians and sworn jurists, together with the parliament and the jury courts, were the political instruments used for the purpose of serving faithfully the axiomatic principles of democracy.

All the above principles of democracy are, in one way or another, embedded in the constitutions of today's democracies around the world; however, they are not being upheld in practice. The political instruments used to serve these principles have been consistently proven to be inadequate or unsuitable. If we continue to follow the same procedure repeatedly, nothing will change. It is said that Einstein, speaking on a different matter (a physical experiment), argued that repeating the same experiment again and again, and expecting a different outcome, is plain stupid! One could further apply these words to our discussion here and argue also that those who invented the present political instruments for serving democracy fell into the same trap, namely of expecting a different outcome, when the political experiments should have shown them otherwise. Most of the harm done is to be traced back to the way the political parties operate. This subject will be dealt extensively further below, where the origins of the specific operational structures of parties will be brought to light.

Democracy, as defined by the general principles and the instruments mentioned above, was not considered to be a result, but a means through which to pursue the welfare of the people. None of these principles or instruments were neglected in any decision-making procedure. They were all included in the process of making decisions, and in the definition itself of the system of government called democracy. **In this sense, ancient Athenian democracy was not a democracy "à la carte," the likes of which we see today everywhere around the globe.** There were exceptions too in the case of ancient democracy as well, but these only resulted from the behavioral habits of those attending the sessions of the citizens' assembly, a place that typically lends itself as the perfect environment for the actions of uncontrolled crowds. After all, the citizens' assembly could pass anything it wanted. It had absolute power. The political leaders at that time – whether democrats or aristocrats – were not elected by any political instrument or by the citizens' assembly, where all citizens over the age of twenty could participate and were eligible to vote. Neither were they selected by the method of sortition. They had emerged as leaders through their successful interventions in the citizens' assembly.

Democracy was not the only system of government used in the city-states of Greece. Sparta, for example, was one of those cities which preferred to govern by oligarchy. The Spartans even engaged in a war with Athens, which lasted over three decades, during democracy's first hundred years. Later, another Greek state, which was organized as a kingdom, the kingdom of Macedonia, would put an end to democracy. In the following period, the Romans were also not on the side of democracy. They chose as their system of government the **Republic**, which was not really a democracy, and which would give way to Imperial Rome not too long thereafter. The term "democracies" would reemerge significantly later with the coming of the Renaissance. Those were all democracies à la carte, however, a political experiment across different European countries, and essentially the result of public pressure, some of which even had the support of the nobility. Since then, we have been living with these forms of democracy which, while somehow improving over the course of time, in no way resembled the type of democracy first implemented in ancient Greece.

### 1.3 Opponents of Democracy

Today, there are many opponents of the type of democracy that was applied in ancient Greece, and their arguments vary. Some critics use Rousseau's argument who, referring with a certain regret to the failure of direct democracy as applied in the city of Geneva, stated that because of the time and effort required for their personal business, the Swiss people had scarcely any time to engage in the running of democracy, whereas the ancient Greeks were relieved of their daily preoccupations by their slaves, and had therefore enough free time to devote to this task. **According to Rousseau, therefore, democracy was invented by the rich Athenians**, which is a doubtful argument, to say the least, coming especially from a figure like Rousseau, and an argument which, in fact, has no connection to reality. Yet it is still being used today by some academics and writers in the West, who adopt Rousseau's claim without undertaking the slightest investigation as to its validity, as though it were a given that, since Rousseau said it, then it must be true. This does not seem to be a very "objective" argument. Or is it perhaps intended to conceal something else? Either way, it is not convincing. **Democracy in Greece succeeded not so much because of the levels of participation, but because of the methods used to select all the different public officials, in a hard struggle between the democrats and the rich conservatives.**

To begin with, during the period of the three-and-a-half centuries when democracy was taking shape as a system of government in ancient Greece, Greece had:

1. Faced and successfully dealt with the critical menace of the Persian invasions.
2. Developed very successful relations with many nations to its East, West, South and North, and it had also developed rich commercial activity.
3. Achieved unique accomplishments in science, philosophy, the arts and letters, architecture and engineering; the Parthenon is testament to

these achievements, in spite of Morosini's detonation of the gunpowder reserves that the Ottomans had stored in this unique monument, and Lord Elgin's removal of fifty carved architectural elements, the famous **metopes**, which supported the Parthenon's structure.

4. Gained ship-building capabilities, especially as regards war ships, which enabled the Greek fleet to take on the Persians successfully (under Themistocles' admiralship for instance).

5. Developed a remarkable tradition in miniature crafts and an impressive exports industry.

**Should we assume that these highly advanced sectors of activity were made possible through slave labor?**

Whatever degree of success one ascribes to ancient democracy, one cannot but acknowledge, beyond any doubt, that this system of government can be very successful; the condition is that the necessary adjustments be made, as required by today's prevailing conditions, thus invalidating Rousseau's and Adam Swift's argument (11).

The ancient Athenian political system worked for three and half centuries, even if it did not always do so in an ideal manner. By making the necessary changes to it, it can work even more successfully especially today. Democracy in ancient Greece was invented and implemented in order to engage with and solve serious problems that the nation faced at the time. In addition to all the arguments presented above, one should also bear in mind that slaves were not a monopoly of ancient Greece. While other countries also had slaves, Greece was the only country where democracy was invented and successfully implemented as a system of government. During the colonial period, the British transported many black people from Africa to America, where they were sold as slaves. Those slaves were used primarily as servants to the rich or as agricultural laborers. Their presence was not the reason why Americans selected the republican system of government. The slaves' condition started to change with the end of the civil war, but meaningful changes only began during the last century, when black people, in an organized manner, especially through participation in the two main political parties, successfully sought to alter their condition. In fact, not only did they succeed in freeing themselves from the chains of slavery, but they also lived to see the day when a black person became the president of the USA.

Other arguments are also being used to justify a widely held opinion which argues that the form of democracy practiced in ancient Greece cannot be used in today's world. This argument is presented as more "sophisticated," as it rests on supposedly "scientific" data, which either refer to the intrinsic nature of humankind, or emphasize the much greater size of the world's population. It is known that humans, in order to survive, had to use all available means, including every form of violence, even when that might cause the death of other human beings. In this context, wars between different tribes were a common feature in the struggle for survival. In line with this intrinsic behavior, humans also possessed a drive to dominate. The results produced by this effort were not all negative, as this struggle also led to progress in various fields of human endeavor. In order to become more efficient, humans, in their struggle to survive, invented many tools, and, most important of all, they developed the ability to control fire.

Certain opponents of democracy claim that because this system seeks to harness these two historical tendencies of humanity, it goes against human nature, and is therefore unsuitable as a model of government. The best we can do, some of them argue, is to confine ourselves to certain less rigid forms of democracy, and such examples can already be seen in some places. In line with this argument, the Western à la carte democracies that took shape in Europe were the result of these human limitations, which required an adjustment of the original model of democracy. Needless to say, the various models of democracy that emerged in this way perfectly suited the forces of the status quo that prevailed throughout this evolutionary process, first in feudalism, and later in capitalism, both of which were (as capitalism still is) hostile to any systemic reform towards true democratic systems of government.

As has been stated earlier, true democracy is also the creator of civilized societies, where the exploitation of others cannot thrive. It is therefore no surprise that educational systems in all à la carte democracies are preoccupied mainly with producing good scientists, doctors, engineers etc., in order to bolster the "miracles" of business growth and profit increase, while neglecting educational sectors that promote a cultured way of life for society, because this goes against the interests of the forces in power. In the long run, this attitude meant that no changes were deemed necessary, despite popular pressures for more meaningful reforms intended to protect the poor from excessive exploitation. Popular pressure of course somehow managed to restrain and even replace strict authoritarian regimes with democracies of some form, and the latter are in any case preferable to the regimes they replaced. Yet all these changes evidently had their cost. They came as a result of hard struggles, and much blood was shed for long periods during catastrophic wars.

The main argument against the implementation of true democracy has to do with the limitations that might arise as a result of the democratic process, which would hinder the development and expression of people's talent and creative forces. They claim that sortition may bring to power persons with a low IQ, whereas elections, they argue, where the people are the judges, protect us from such a catastrophe.

However, the above argument is not supported by what happens in real life.

All the candidates who take part in elections today are volunteers; they are not being drafted by force.

For a party member to acquire the title of candidate in any political party certain conditions must be met: the candidate must have the blessings of the party's leadership, or of the strong cliques that mushroom within political parties, or, better yet, of a center or centers with influence over public opinion, to mention a few. It also helps if a candidate has a lot of money, as it helped Donald Trump become president of the USA. These types of required pre-conditions for one to become a candidate constitute an impressive set of con-straints, which restrict considerably the number and the quality of volunteers who are likely to be candidates.

No preconditions, such as competence, knowledge, character or experi-ence, are set as a requirement for one to become a candidate. It suffices that someone's father was president or congressman, senator or representative, or what have you. There are those who argue that the people will be the ultimate judges of all these fine points. On the surface, it would appear to be so. The people are the judges at the ballot, but everyone knows that most of them are not free agents. And when they were, as they claim, the judges, they have also been proven to be very bad judges. One must think of cases such as, for exam-ple, the election to power of Hitler, Mussolini and many others.

As regards, however, the use of sortition for the selection of holders of public office, quite the opposite holds true.

Here too the set of potential candidates only refers to volunteers.

In forming the set of **potential candidates**, from which one obtains, by the use of sortition, the office holders for the different political instruments of the party, or the candidate list for parliament or for local government councils, there is only one requirement, namely, that the candidates meet the formal requirements for the job in question, besides being of sound mind. If the candidate is a member of the party, he has no need of endorsement by the leadership or by any other center of influence. He becomes a candidate just by sheer luck. He is totally independent from all sorts of obligations to anyone. He is also free of any collusion, because he is to serve for one term only and is, therefore, in no need to search for opportunities to renew his term, a process which usually produces interdependence and/or collusion. These are the representatives that we so desperately need in true democracies. This kind of representative elicits the so-called **conscience vote.**

Candidates selected by sortition do not have to worry during the election process that they may be facing a hostile network inside or outside the party, because they are not the result of the preferences and support of the leadership, or of any party cliques, or centers of influence, within or outside the party. All this web of dependency and collusion is now rendered obsolete and redundant: candidates will no longer feel a need for it, because of the use of sortition, and because there are no renewals of term any longer. In this manner, more members will be willing to declare their interest in being included in the actual set of volunteers, from which, through sortition, they may be selected for a position. In cases where an election will follow, as is the case for members of parliament, and because of the process of double sortition, candidates are no longer required to spend money for the election campaign (the first sortition determines the electoral list and the second, which takes place after the election, determines the ranking of each candidate on the list, and, of course, the specific candidates elected, which depends on the percentage of votes won by the party). The only money spent by any party for the campaign are the funds provided by the state. No other financial support to political parties is allowed. This means that the higher the number of potential candidates there are in the set from which applicants for a position (public office) or candidates on the electoral list (parliament) will be drawn by lot, the higher the probability for competent and decent citizens to be selected. One should keep in mind that many serious citizens do not want to get involved in practices where collusion and competition between the cliques are the means by which they can arrive to such political positions.

This process can also ensure political equality among the candidates, and it can ensure balanced electoral lists as regards gender and race.

One can clearly see which of these two processes truly serves the axiomatic principles of democracy, while at the same time upholding the axiom of meritocracy in politics. One can definitely argue that real democracy produces cultured societies, while also faithfully serving meritocracy.

Plato also had certain objections as regards the way decisions were taken during his time, arguing that these decisions should be taken by people with the highest intelligence, who would need to be selected by some form of system (yet what system is there, which can be free of collusion? For that is the problem…). This system would choose the most able candidate from among a group, rather than appointing candidates through election or sortition. In a true democratic process, selecting someone less talented than others can occur, but the chances of this happening, when using sortition, are far lower than in the case of elected officials, as **the specific prerequisites for any political position exclude candidates who do not meet them from the set of volunteers from which the draw is made. In the case of ancient Athenian democracy, it also did not matter as much, because the politicians were not tasked with implementing the decisions taken in the assemblies.** This was assigned to specialists, who were elected by the citizens' assembly, where the voters were almost totally independent from any influence other than that of being swayed by what was said by those who spoke in the assembly. One should keep in mind that specialists were also elected for a single term. The only exception to this rule was the election of the generals. They also, therefore, did not have any incentive to try and prolong or renew their term with the help of others. The only possible legal offence was bribing a voter, but in those days it would have been even more expensive for the bribe-giver, for he would have had to bribe a lot of voters, something that would not be necessary in our days, since it seems to be sufficient for modern centers of influence to aim only for the top tier of party officials. If any risk of misconduct were to emerge, however, provisions were in place via the control exercised by the citizens' assembly, which, judging from the results, must have been very strict, and doing a very good job most of the time. These control mechanisms were always available and rigorously applied. In ancient Athens, democracy could only be overpowered by an external force. During the three-and-a-half centuries during which it thrived, there were cases when internal forces did manage to suspend the operation of democracy, only to see it return with renewed strength.

Finally, there is another form of government that has been presented as being democratic (and is still being claimed to be so): it was promoted as such in Europe and elsewhere, especially since the appearance of Marxist formulas, opening the way for the government of the proletariat. Generally, in any given society, the have-nots tend to outnumber considerably the haves, so there are always many more people who are poor than rich members of a society. This situation has been (and continues to be) exploited by the so-called Marxists of all sorts, who, operating in an environment created by deficient democracies, promote the rule of the proletariat as a democratic government, and, of course, claim to be democrats themselves. Their premise is that proletarians always outnumber the rest of the population, and consequently such a government must be constantly in power according to the provisions of democracy. When this is not the case, they – the proletarians – assume that they should, by any means available to them, seize power, even using undemocratic methods that may include the use of violence. Such governments have appeared in our times, either through elections or through revolts. None of them implemented what they preached, and with time they collapsed. Also, none of them had any relation whatsoever with true democratic government. In fact, some of them were very brutal, establishing terrible dictatorships, engulfing both the natural environment and humankind in chaos. As a result, the world reaches a state where two classes constantly clash with each other, the capitalists (where one may include also the socialists of any kind, for the word social is all-inclusive in a **real** democracy, which has no need for socialists), and the proletarians; all "democratic" process is delimited by and expended between these two groups.

Societies are thereby forced to live constantly in an environment of collision and destruction, thus being kept in a condition of primitive barbarity, and, unquestionably, far from any cultured state enabled by the provisions of democracy. Thus the only contribution of these two catastrophic forces is to keep humanity in its primitive model of action, and thus to keep what Freud calls "misery" out of humankind's struggle for survival – in other words, to keep humans in good company with their primitive and barbaric basic instincts for survival, and perpetually free from the "chains" of a true culture, as described by **Freud**. The latter, when referring to human nature, stated: **Culture is the source of misery in man's nature,** for it is culture that resists the dangerous aggressive nature of man, a resistance that may lead to man's "taming and domestication." **Therefore, for those who oppose democracy, their enemy**

**is indeed a cultured society of the type democracy strived to produce in ancient Greece.** Culture works against the dangerous violent tendencies of human beings, resulting in the weakening of this aggressive behavior by intrinsically creating an administrative force that acts automatically, and succeeds in taming and reducing this violent tendency.

Speaking of culture, one must clarify from the outset that this term signifies simply a way of living (5). Culture is not enshrined in the impressive buildings the archeologists uncover with pride for the purpose of establishing, as they tell us, the degree of culture attained by the builders. If we did not know that the Parthenon was indeed the achievement of a deeply cultured society, no archeologist would have been able to tell us more than the fact that the monument has been constructed by skillful people who, however, may have had nothing in common with the members of such a cultured society. Nor is culture the sum of a society's scientific and technological accomplishments, for in that case Hitler would have been first in line to be pronounced a cultured citizen! We should not mistake as culture the specialist knowledge acquired by a person through hard work and many years of studying the arts – music, painting, etc. – the sciences, and other disciplines. All these have nothing to do with culture. They are simply associated with school learning and special training. **The traits of a cultured person are not special knowledge, but his or her conduct towards their fellow humans and the environment. Special knowledge may help accelerate this conversion into a cultured individual, just as it can contribute to creating a monster.**

## 1.4 Forces Supporting Democracy

A cultured society of a highly advanced level can only be produced by a true democratic system of government that rests upon the foundations mentioned earlier. The efforts of a democratic government to achieve these objectives can certainly **be assisted** by certain religions that are founded on principles – commandments – requiring from its followers to make, among other things, personal sacrifices or, for those who have the possibility, to share their possessions with the poor. The incentive for the followers of such religions to observe these commandments derives from the central aim these followers have, namely, to save their souls by doing good deeds during their lifetimes. This is another element of human nature that we should not ignore in our assessments. Killing people, for instance, in order to save one's soul, which is the premise of jihad, has clearly no relation to any god. Bad or jealous gods were already in "existence" at the time of the ancient Greeks. Their numbers started at thirty thousand and were slowly reduced to twelve. Today, almost all "gods" expect from their followers only the sacrificing of values in order to save their souls, rather than killing for the sake of saving one's own skin (or soul)! By contrast, when Marxist revolutionaries include such acts among their practices, they admit that they are doing any necessary killing only for the benefit of others, and not for themselves (the saving of souls is not on any Marxist menu); a jihad fighter, however, does the killing to save his own soul. Quite a sacrifice! "Religions" which provide such incentives to their followers are akin to criminal mafias that exploit poor souls, and therefore have no place whatsoever on this planet.

In line with these arguments, it is also necessary to point out that the separation of state and church (religion) promoted by certain forms of government deprives democracy of forces that contribute to its efforts to strengthen those elements that constitute a cultured society. For example, the Ten Commandments of the Judeo-Christian religion are loaded with cultural content, and democracy needs followers of such religions that practice these commandments faithfully. After all, that is exactly what democracy is trying to accomplish, namely, to have citizens who are mindful of their fellow citizens, and who uphold the principles of democracy. Therefore, instead of promoting the separation of the church from the state, it is more important to invite church leaders to support the democratic government, and to contribute to its efforts to build a truly cultured society. In effect, governments should give church leaders responsibility over the affairs of the state as far as the conduct of citizens towards their fellow human beings is concerned. This implies of course that church leaders should limit their activities to what their religion expects from them, namely the salvation of their followers' souls. This presupposes, of course, that they should at least be able to save their own soul before trying to save the souls of others. A democratic society should therefore have a say in the question of who is fit to become a church leader. A strict adherence to, and practice of religious principles should be the only criterion by which any member of the congregation should be assessed when wanting to become a church leader. Religious leaders who mingle in politics and make statements that have no relation to the principles of their religion, are either servants of capitalism or hungry for power. Their intent is to promote their own personal agendas and not those of god.

Apart from the efforts that a responsible state and its church leaders should make towards creating a truly democratic society, the most important agent of such a change is an appropriate system of education. Such a system should not limit its activities to training good professionals of any kind, but it should rather evince the same interest and effort that it invests in the training of the best engineers, doctors and scientists, in conveying to the members of society the knowledge required for running a democracy. It should nurture, through narratives based on the axiomatic principles of democracy, strong and healthy citizens. Paul Collier (12), in his book *The future of Capitalism*, mentions three types of such narratives – namely those focusing on belonging, obligation and causality – which complement one another in order to create a network of reciprocal obligations. These narratives make it possible for a member of society to make the transition from the self-centeredness that is characteristic of economy-driven individuals, to the social awareness of obligation-driven persons. The latter recognize themselves as part of a communal "we," whereby people view each other not through the prism of fear or indifference, but through the premise of mutual regard. In other words, through the appropriate narratives one can persuade man to accept alternate ways of fulfilling his dreams, if, of course, he can overcome his intrinsic nature through culture. Thus, while a society's traditions are certainly important, so is scientific knowledge, which should not be overlooked or ignored in favor of traditional values. New scientific research, for example in psychology, provides knowledge that can produce major breakthroughs in the field of children's upbringing. Parents who are able to know how important is the first year in the life of their newborn child, and what they should do to raise mentally and physically healthy children, contribute immensely to the effort the rest of society is making towards promoting and protecting a democratic system of government, of which the cultural element is one of its most important intrinsic components. This knowledge should be provided to all young people in society, and at all levels of an educational system.

## 1.5 Supporters Who Are Still Skeptical About Democracy's Return

After all we have said, and despite the benefits that a system of democratic government can deliver, there is significant skepticism even among proponents of democracy. Their claim is based on the fact that true democracy has at least two very powerful enemies: Capitalism, and dictatorships of all kinds, whether overt or veiled; and as long as these enemies exist, no progress can be made towards a true democratic system of government. The main argument of believers in democracy who are, nonetheless, skeptical of its pragmatic potential is like that made by economists regarding the marginal effect in the domain of production of goods or services. Their question is: why spend so much effort to improve the situation so little?

The answer to these and other arguments that seek to minimize the societal benefits of democracy is that these benefits are not only significant for the vast majority at least of the members of any society, but at the same time, they are **necessary for the survival of humankind.** Apparently, to most capitalists, these benefits are not, at first sight, very convincing. To them, it is more attractive to find low-cost labor or to replace workers with robots, and to lay off millions of people, mainly those aged over the age of 50, who will then join the constantly growing numbers of the unemployed. In the long run, however, this will lead to a contraction of their beloved market. Let us hope that ultimately, and with the assistance of the democratic system of government, many more capitalists will switch sides and become social partners, as a result of better trust between the rich and the poor. We have seen a list of very rich people of late, asking their governments to tax them more for the purpose of helping the victims of the Covid-19 pandemic.

In addition, the more the security issue becomes problematic for members of a society over time, the more these citizens will join arms and, on a collective basis, will try to deal with, and overcome the threats to their security. From time immemorial, the issue of security has always been for any human group the priority to require resolution. Only when this is resolved successfully, can then the next problem in order of priority for society be addressed, which is the issue of economics, namely finding a fair or unfair point of equilibrium in the economic relations between its members. These are all the means and arguments (short of resorting to the use of violence of course) that one can use to convince a capitalist to join forces with the poor. The more prominent argument in this effort concerns the running of the democratic system of government, which, by virtue of its nature, continuously enhances the level of trust between a capitalist and someone who is poor, or, collectively, the working class. This is accomplished through the mechanisms of the democratic system of government, whereby the cultural level of the members of society concerned is continuously being raised, thus improving at the same time the quality of interaction between citizens, and the overall vision each citizen has, and is striving to accomplish, for society as a whole.

Today we are faced with two basic camps: the capitalist faction, and the proponents of the dictatorship of the proletariat, along the lines proposed by Marx. There are of course other forms of dictatorship, namely the religious and the fascist. However, both types of dictatorship are in happy tandem with capitalism, and, as things stand, not much can be done at present in that regard. Humanity can only hope for some improvements in cases where the capitalist model of production operates in **à la carte democracies.** In countries operating under this restricted form of democracy, one can, by using rational and convincing arguments, rather than violence or threats of any kind, improve the status of the working class, as compared to the capitalist model of production, from within the framework of a true democratic system.

On a global scale, capitalism is at present the dominant force, and, therefore the dominant model of production, and, as a result, productive relations tend to go from bad to worse. **The economist Thomas Piketty (13) foresees that during the twenty-first century, conditions for the working class will deteriorate to the point of becoming similar to those that existed in the nineteenth century, in spite of all the efforts and the blood spilt by this class and its leaders.** The experts' conclusion is also that the working class with its proletarian dictatorships, with or without violence, has gotten nowhere, and that in fact the situation for the working class all over the world is worsening. It is therefore no wonder that the communist parties see their influence among the working classes in the Western world waning continuously. The leaders of the working class, wherever they have taken power through violence, or have come to power through elections, have failed miserably, for the simple reason that leftist or Marxist governments, because of their ideology, lose or squander their most important partner, namely, capital – it either flees abroad to safety, or is destroyed through Marxist policies, which do not take into consideration the fact that wealth is generated by companies producing goods and services that can be sold at a profit in a, hopefully free, competitive market. Needless to say, salaries for the working people in the profit-making companies are kept at levels which allow these companies to stay competitive. If these important constraints are not honored, sooner or later this will lead to the collapse of the entire enterprise, including workers' salaries. Up until now, the experience of well-meaning leftist or Marxist governments has been very negative, because they were either ignorant of, or over-looked these constraints. It goes without saying that in the case of not well-intentioned leftist or Marxist governments, the evolution of the revolution becomes a nightmare for the working class, as well as for the revolution's more romantic leaders.

Such revolutions turn out to resemble the worst dictatorships that human-ity has ever witnessed, for reasons that are to be found in human nature. Recent research also finds that the IQ of a society's members, which is determined not by birth, but as a result of training, is like the spectrum of light. The variations in IQ and in interests among the members of a society is essential for the evo-lutionary process to occur. Ironically, and depending, of course, on the existing conditions, what is essential for the evolution of humanity can turn out to be a nightmare, instead of a blessing, as has been attested on repeated occasions dur-ing the course of humanity. These developments have provided plenty of ex-perience for societies, and this historical experience is the reason why working-class people put less and less faith in the proclamations of leftists or Marxist leaders. Therefore, the argument of reverting back to democracy gains more and more ground amongst the working class, but there are still many dif-ficulties present in the so-called democracies à la carte, where many pressure groups are in operation under the cover of constitutional provisions and laws, or government "assistance," all of which promise their members what leftist and Marxist governments have failed to deliver. The result of the actions of these pressure groups is that important decisions about the future of a country are being taken outside the deliberations of parliaments, and often in secrecy. These negotiations are conducted between political parties and the pressure groups, on the premise that members of the group will then vote for the party concerned in the coming elections, if the party agrees to support their demands in parliament, a process that usually takes the form of blackmail. This approach by pressure groups is also used with members of parliament and government ministers and employing the same tactics: I will vote for you if you do some-thing for us in return. **This process leads to inequalities among the citizens in every society.** This issue will be discussed in more detail further below, and some ideas will be presented on how to combat the unethical practices of po-litical parties, ministers, lawmakers, and pressure groups of all kinds.

Based on all that is happening in the so-called democracies around the world, it is not difficult to conclude that these systems are not oriented towards a just democracy or a democracy for all, rich and poor. These democracies, if one also takes into account the way public information is generated, belong to certain powerful economic and other centers, which direct all the political (and of course economic) activity for the purpose of serving their own interests in the best way possible. **If people in countries where these pseudo-democracies operate want to see better days, they must become involved in the workings of political parties, and not in the operations of pressure groups. And, by using the meagre opportunities these democracies are offering, they should be able to combat these unethical practices – many of which are illegal or unconstitutional to say the least – from within rather than outside parliament.** The position taken by many citizens who want to see the implementation of these changes is that **it is not possible to change anything, or that "one cannot fight city hall,"** and that it is therefore best to stay clear of any involvement. They hence end up serving in the very best way the private vested interests that citizens in fact want to see eliminated for good.

Even though these pseudo-democracies fail to serve the citizens' interests, they nevertheless do provide possibilities for people to push for and even to succeed in promoting the desired changes. The key to success is participation in the activities of those political parties, **whose programs include the desired changes, and whose internal workings use the methods of real democracy.** Another option is to start from scratch. We will explore this aspect more closely in a separate chapter on political parties. Briefly stated, while some professors are wasting theirs and our time telling us how democracies die, or teaching people the workings of government, or presenting ways of combating the system, instead of changing the system, they may want to spend their time promoting real democracies. If we use **Aristotle's** categories, the types of democracy we have today would be classed as oligarchic systems of government.

# Chapter Two

## 2.1 First Steps Towards Improving
## the Functioning of Today's "Democracies"

In the previous chapter, we learned what system of government is defined as a democracy, and why today's democracies, even though they are operating in the name of democracy, in reality fall short of being one. We also got to know some of those who are in favor of this type of democracy, and those who are opposed to it. In this chapter, we will outline the first steps towards improving democracies for the purpose of arriving at a true democratic society in the long run, one which will serve the entire people, and we hope that some of the opponents of this democracy, whom we investigated in the first chapter, will switch sides and join forces with us. However, before doing that, we need to learn a little more about what we have in mind when invoking the term direct democracy, since, whatever we decide to do, it will not be an implementation of Athenian democracy in its original form: it will instead have to be an intelligent use and application of the critical tools crafted by the Athenians, adapted to today's conditions. The objective, of course, will be to establish a democratic system of government which will work in a truly just way for all.

## 2.2 Why Did the Ancient Athenians Use Certain Political
## Instruments in Order to Serve the Principles of Democracy?

Before we can answer this question, we need to examine certain other matters that concern the choice of the political instruments of democracy created by the Athenians. These have to do with the reactions of human beings when faced with specific situations, from the perspective of intrinsic human nature.

As we have seen in the first chapter, humans, following their nature, had to work together from the start in their effort to deal with threats to their physical survival, and jointly with other human beings facing the same threats, a necessity that subsequently led to the formation of tribal communities. The historic outcome of this is that people facing threats or opportunities work collectively and make collective decisions, especially when all members of the tribe enjoy the benefits gained through the collective action that has been decided. If securing their physical survival had not been a problem at the time, collective action probably would not have arisen at all. We see this kind of conduct being exhibited by humans during the transition from primitive types of tribes to well-developed ones, when the more intelligent, or physically stronger tribal members either abandon them, or took over as their leaders or kings. In the recent past, we have seen this kind of evolution in all the cases of the dictatorship of the proletariat. One can speak here of a paradox, whereby progress in a certain direction, which sums up the overall evolution of human beings, turns out to be detrimental to the evolution of the overall welfare of a society, and of course its culture. This phenomenon emerges as a result of the system of government. In a democratic system of government this phenomenon tends to gradually disappear, as a more cultured society is being put in its place. At least that is the lesson one learns by studying the evolution of Athenian democracy.

Now, as we know, one thing brings another, because once the collective actions of a tribe had been dealt with successfully, as regards threats to physical survival, its members went further, and undertook additional activities, primarily of an economic nature, namely collectively securing food and other items they needed for the members of the tribe, initially through hunting, and later on in other ways that led to the development of agriculture. At that time, the cohesion of the members of the tribe started to loosen, because the basic conditions for survival had been met quite successfully. At this stage, other additional interests of individual members, especially of the more competent ones, started to emerge. These types of interest were satisfied through the actions of each individual separately, rather than collectively, and thus the seeds of differentiation among the members of the tribe were planted, due to these additional activities based on different interests, and due to the difference in

IQ among the members of the tribe. Evolution and development brought new forms of societal organization, some of them through unpleasant events, including bloody wars. These different social conditions are encountered today in almost every form of organized group, and of course in all of today's democracies around the globe. Against this historical background, we can assume that collective decisions, and of course collective actions, are feasible, especially if the road to attaining our individual aims is made much easier by working together, than if each member of the group acts individually – provided that the members of the organized group in question obtain a fair share of the benefits accrued by collective action. According to Freud, the cultural elements that are present in a society reflect a specific way of living for its members: these cultural elements create an intrinsic control mechanism inside every member of that society, which in practical terms tames the aggressive nature of human beings. If we accept this position, then we can assume that under certain conditions, collective decisions can be made, and actions can be taken, towards a way of living analogous to that created for its members by ancient Athenian democracy, and without restricting the citizens' talent for creative and entrepreneurial activities. Such conditions, to begin with, must be reflected in the stated aims of the constitution, which guarantees the safeguarding of the rights of all members of society, and binds each member, without any exception, to specific responsibilities.

It then remains for us to define those conditions which will ensure that the necessary collective decisions and actions are taken by the members of that society. Some of these conditions will obviously be related to the existing form of societal organization, in a way that will dictate what should be allowed and what not. Naturally, determining what actions are permissible or not should, in many cases, result automatically, without there being a need to carry out any checks in person.

The organizational model of ancient Athens was based on the existence of tribes in the area around the city. The clever Athenian reformers did not think of abolishing the tribes, but decided to work with them and within them, right where the two main political currents existed and were fighting with each other – the democrats, coming mainly from the coastal areas, and the wealthy, who hailed mostly from the mainland of Attica; of course, the ingenious reformers never thought of abolishing the political currents – the political parties – of that time. Accordingly, if we want to succeed today, we must work with what is available now. Each of today's democracies has a constitution, and there are political parties. This is our real world, and this is the world we have to reform. It is worth mentioning this, considering that many political amateurs, when writing articles or books, and without having the slightest idea of what needs to be done, propose that we should embark on quite the opposite way to the one taken by the Athenians. They prefer to act the revolutionary, and may be inspired by Che Guevara in their bedrooms, and every now and then they may hold ancient style symposia, where they plan their next abortive campaign. In Greece today, there are some small groups acting in a way like those horizontal grassroots movements, which they take to represent the citizens' assemblies of ancient Athenian democracy! Some of them play the role of the tribes, preparing for the application of direct democracy in exactly the same way as the ancient Athenians, but starting and ending their deliberations with slogans such as "down with the parties and the constitution." Alas, they are walking down the path of disaster for their next revolution! It should be born in mind that in the Athenian democracy all power was vested in the citizens' assembly. It was not a citizens' assembly that put requests to the executive power or to the parliament and waited for the changes to happen. The citizens' assembly was the power. This is emphasized here because we see initiatives being taken around the world by organized groups playing the role of citizens' assembly and expecting the miracle to happen. These types of action are also encouraged by certain writings which promote such activities. Later, more will be said about these practices, which will not in the end produce the desired results: instead, they will rather produce a great many disappointments, which will lead many citizens to withdraw to a state of inaction.

Education and certain religions, as has already been said in the previous chapter, can contribute to the efforts society is making to endow its members with certain cultural characteristics, and as we have seen, they can effectively exert control over people's aggressive nature towards their fellow human beings. These two very important social agents are necessary, but not enough in themselves in order to arrive at the desired result, even if the whole process were to evolve perfectly. It is important to acquire an appropriate form of societal organization. The aim of the whole effort is to enable the development of a system of government that will satisfy in practical terms, and with the least expenditure of resources of any kind, the stated principles: providing its members the necessary benefits through which the cumulative result will be achieved – namely, the welfare of all members of society. **Thus, it is important to define the models for the organization and operation of political parties, the government, the executive power, local government, the judiciary, the models of production, and the way members of society are being comprehensively informed about all the issues that concern them, especially in the area of political conduct and the actions of those in power.**

## 2.3 Issues Affecting the Structure and Operation of an Organization

As has already been stated in the previous chapter, one important feature of ancient Athenian democracy was its direct model. This meant that all male citizens over the age of twenty were legally entitled to participate in the deliberations of the citizens' assembly and, by law, had the right to speak and vote. In this way, all participating citizens were involved in making decisions, and, through their vote, they approved or disapproved proposals for laws, foreign and defense policies, and development programs. Those who participated could moreover know at any point after the vote whether affairs were progressing according to the decisions that had been made by the citizens' assembly. This inbuilt control mechanism was an important driving force towards ensuring that actions would be taken in accordance with the decisions. At the time, the number of citizens participating in the assembly's deliberations could be well over six thousand when the matters to be discussed were deemed very important. Considering that Athens had between 20,000 to 45,000 men of voting age (the higher number corresponds to periods of peace), we understand that a full turnout, with the participation of all male citizens over the age of twenty, was never achieved, for reasons explained in the first chapter. Yet, and despite rather poor participation, direct democracy worked well, most of the time, judging from the results that it produced. One might even venture to claim that the lower the participation, the more effective were the sessions of the assemblies.

As far as the quality of the decisions is concerned, one may be quite skeptical about them, since the social or geographical ratios in the group synthesis of the participants may not have been sufficient for the assembly to be genuinely representative of the population of the city-state. **What is important to stress is that direct Athenian democracy was actually a representative democracy.** The quality of the decisions was also very much dependent on the procedures used to reach them.

The same, of course, can be said for today's decisions all over the world. The way governance is organized today, in most nations that embrace some form of democratic government, is very much prone to squandering resources of all kinds. Priorities are most of the time not so much aligned with the interests of the people, but rather with those dictated mainly by the capitalist model of production as we know it. As a result of this dysfunctional democratic process, we witness many paradoxical results. Meanwhile, many people still accept the way today's governments operate, mainly because elections are being held. There are, however, as many people who don't even take the trouble to vote. They believe that the current way of carrying on with things cannot continue. They blame for that the way elections are being held. Nonetheless, people's obsession with elections is strong, and cannot be stamped out overnight. People believe that when they vote, the choices they are making are their own—something which is clearly not true for many of them, however. This obviously suits the politicians quite well. Thus, if we hope to make any progress towards some form of improved democracy, we must take these reservations seriously into account. Hence, we must become more creative, more inventive in designing an adequate set of provisions for an enhanced, functional democracy, no matter its imperfections, by making good use of technology, and being armed with enough determination and patience.

In any case, before we may proceed along those lines, we need to be sure that the people are willing to belong to such a societal union. The dissemination, therefore, of information to the citizens in a society will be helpful, in the long run, and, in that respect, organizations promoting democratic ideas are welcome and should be supported.

## 2.4 The World is Blessed. Some Helpful Proposals Already Exist

Certain proposals are already being circulated around the globe by various groups or foundations, and even by some specialists or think tanks, aiming at the improvement of today's democracies. One of these proposes the election of 15 to 30 thousand candidates, who will constitute the reservoir from which we should select by sortition the required number of members of parliament, the cabinet and the prime minister, as well as any other public officials who may be required (14). However, the fact that an election is involved for obtaining the reservoir of candidates makes the process, under the present conditions, very vulnerable to collusion and corruption from outside centers of influence. These centers can simply promote their candidates and fill the reservoir with them. They have the means to accomplish this. Yet let us assume that we do accept this way of proceeding for the purpose of ameliorating today's democracies. How does one arrive at the point where this process can begin? Today's democracies have constitutions, governments, parliaments and a lot of other things, all of which may find themselves opposed to such a process. Does anyone think that this may come through some revolution? For it is certain that no establishment will welcome it by rolling out the red carpets. This solution is therefore in need of some very difficult preconditions for it to be implemented, which do not exist.

The most popular idea, which enjoys a certain support by people living in Western democratic countries, is the citizens' assembly, like the one the ancient Athenians used to have in order to run the affairs of their democracy. It is a very catchy concept to many people, for it implies that the people are in power. Nonetheless, this idea runs against the same problems as the previous one, namely that for one to be able to apply it, the preconditions of the first proposal must be fulfilled here as well. The type of citizens' assemblies that exist and operate today, exist either in some professor's lab, or belong to the type that operates like the famous horizontal grassroots movements. In those organizations, members vote in their assemblies on a few declarations on various issues, such as the protection of the environment, human rights, bringing certain wars to an end, and many others; these they send later to those who control power, asking them, or demanding of them, to promote their resolutions, or else they will not have their vote. Such actions, however, no matter how good or necessary they may be, have had very limited success. These citizens' assemblies work like the famous pressure groups, some of which, having more money and better organizational structures, oppose very effectively the ideas promoted by these citizens' assemblies. One thing that must be kept in everyone's mind is that the citizens' assembly of ancient Athens had all the political power under its exclusive control. It was the decision-making body, and not a pressure group or grassroots movement.

Because of the popularity enjoyed by the idea of a citizens' assembly, it is important to clarify the actual meaning that it had in practice in ancient times. It is true that all powers were vested in the citizens' assembly. This is the place where all decisions were made. The citizens' assembly passed laws, elected the ten generals, took all the decisions on foreign policy and defense issues, and made all other decisions that had to do with the governance of a country. The decisions were taken on the principle of a ruling majority. All participating citizens over the age of twenty years had the right to speak and vote. For certain decisions, having to do with the punishment meted out to a citizen or to political leaders, or with the approval of the naturalization of a non-Athenian, the required upper limit of participation for the decision to be valid was six thousand. There was no lower limit for the assembly to take decisions concerning other matters, while participation was voluntary. All these were stipulated by laws of the Athenian city-state. The citizens' assembly was a pivotal political instrument that aimed at satisfying all the axiomatic principles of democracy. All these principles have been already stated further above. These were the intensions (and they were in fact very good intentions) of the citizens' assembly, but, as regards certain issues, they remained just that: good intentions. In practice, other things were also happening, which bore no relation to the axiomatic principles of democracy.

Before we come to those other things, let us examine the validity of the claim of those who refer to the Athenian democracy as a direct democracy. To begin with, the participation of the eligible citizens in the deliberations of the assembly was throughout very poor. It was already mentioned that participation ranged usually between several hundred to three thousand out of a total of eligible voters which ranged between twenty to forty thousand, depending on the period (4, 8). Based on these levels of participation, one can only speak of a representative democracy, and not a direct one. In fact, because the participation consisted only of those who were able to participate, one may conclude that even this participation was not of the required standard as regards geographic and social background. Therefore, the only thing that one may say, based on the situation described, is that the Athenian democracy was at best an unsatisfactory representative (and not a direct) democracy.

Other shortcomings of this representative democracy have to do with the form of the deliberations taking place in the citizens' assembly and the way decisions were taken.

According to the rules of the deliberations, every participant could take the floor and speak, on equal terms as regards time, on any subject of the agenda he wished to address. This right was provided by the law of "isegoria" (equal speaking time). In practice, however, this did not happen. The floor was usually dominated by the specialist orators and generally by citizens who were educated and knew what to say in each case. Ordinary citizens, such as farmers or sailors, would not dare take the floor (1, 8, 6). Anyone from that latter category who ventured to take the floor would be booed until they stepped down (see Aristotle, *The Athenian Constitution*, Sinclair, Cartledge and others). For these reasons, ordinary citizens generally avoided to claim the floor. This meant that some voices representing different interests would never be heard.

At the conclusion of the discussion on each issue, a vote was taken. Voters voted for or against by show of hand, and the total number of votes was estimated, not counted. Now, assuming that participation in the open-air citizens' assembly was as high as a couple of thousands, and knowing that microphones and speakers were not yet invented, anyone with any amount of experience can easily deduce that the proceedings of the assembly did not reflect a political instrument capable of promoting all the axiomatic principles of democracy. During the proceedings of the assembly, according to the sources (1, 8, 4) there was plenty of clamor, coming from different groups—mainly the democrats or the conservatives, or, even worse, the cliques attached to some prominent figures. This phenomenon was a habitual one. At that time there were also no political parties of the type we have today, and the voting results would often be contested. Today some of these problems can be overcome, but the question of who would be in a position to really influence the participants of such an assembly into forming opinions on the basis of his statements can be, to judge from the results, easily answered. Today we know, even on a political party basis, the role played by the different internal cliques in the decision-making process, and how much these cliques influence the end results. One can imagine what will happen in an assembly where all different parties take place.

To get a more vivid sense of things, a small sample of what can happen is the scenes we witness during "discussions" in national parliaments. We know from sources (1, 8, 4) that in the direct democracy of ancient Athens those who always had the upper hand during the deliberations of the assembly were the aristocrats and the rich. Which is like what is happening today. This can easily be seen by examining the results of elections for the selection of specialists to public office during that time. They all came from the aristocrats and the rich. This proves that the people were not at all in power, even though they had, by law, the right to vote. This is exactly what is happening in our times. Of course, some of the specialists elected by the assembly at the time were prominent figures, such as Pericles, and through their policies, and as a result of this happy coincidence, the golden age of the Athenian democracy was rendered possible. These prominent figures transformed the city-state of Attica-Athens into an oasis within that wider geographical area, while others, such as the generals Miltiades and Themistocles, through their victories against the Persian invaders, gave to Athenian democracy the fame it well deserved. One can surely define the situation during that period as the earliest phase of the capitalist model of production. After all, Marx did tell his comrades that not everything created by capitalism was bad. In those times, instead of the mechanized production chains, they had large farms or small manufacturing plants, where the role of the machine was taken up by slaves and the working class. The picture described above also implies that the citizens' assembly was very much exposed to collusion and corruption.

The world has never been angelic. It is not angelic today. The question therefore arises: can a citizens' assembly reclaim the place it had in ancient times, when it was vested with total power? And if the answer is yes, how would it be possible to discuss and decide policies on very sensitive issues, such as foreign policy or matters of defense, out in the open? Technology makes it possible today to transfer information to enemies or just to political opponents instantly. The citizens' assembly deliberated for approximately 35 to 40 days, and for the rest of the year the 500 parliamentarians took on an executive and supervising role. 50 members of parliament, all coming from one tribe, and with a tenure that lasted only a year, ran the business of parliament and government daily. Parliament oversaw the work of the specialists who, one might say, were similar to cabinet ministers.

Another important element in the citizens' assembly was that those who voted for or against a proposal were able to totally hide themselves in the crowd. They were not part of a political party, which would then bear a cumulative political responsibility and liability based on the type of proposals it was putting forward for vote in the assembly.

Clearly, and based on prior historical experience, as outlined above, the option of a citizens' assembly as a future system of government would no longer be suitable. However, the citizens' assembly is a good way to educate the public about the democratic process, and a setting where specialists in different fields can be invited so that they may present matters of concern to citizens. Through a discussion of these issues, citizens can acquire, in addition to knowledge, also experience on how different issues should be discussed, since some form of a citizens' assembly will be required in the system that will be proposed later, regarding the organizational structure of our future political parties.

## 2.5 Proposals for Improving US Politics

At this point it would be of interest to examine some other approaches that are being promoted by certain specialists in this field, which, according to them, are best suited for the USA, as well as for some other nations. For example, they claim that in the US emphasis should be given in informing the public on different issues, while stressing also how important it is for people to go and vote. Basically, they accept the current political system as being sound in principle and use the same political instruments to get different results! These instruments, however, are being used also by their opponents, who have, moreover, more means, better institutional structures, and plenty of money to fight back. As a result, one sees no forthcoming changes.

It is important to look at the case of America in greater detail in order to understand the problem, so that one might propose solutions that can bring about real changes there.

Lawrence Lessing, Harvard professor of law and author of several publications on the factors that undermine the workings of democracy, is one case to look at, for he enumerates the different failings that destabilize, according to him, democracy in the USA. In his book, *They don't represent us, reclaiming our democracy*, published by Day St., an imprint of William Morrow, Professor Lessing summarizes most of the evils to be found in US "democracy" (15), and proposes actions to claim democracy back. **For anyone who wants to be more informed about American politics, this book is worth reading.**

Before mentioning some of his ideas, it should be said at the outset that America is far from being considered a country where democracy is the system at work, if we follow Aristotle's definition. Yet the Harvard professor in his writings gives the impression that the US has had democracy all along, and it is only now that it no longer has it. This view might have been adopted because, as he says, "From the beginning, theorists of democracy have understood that there are two very different ways for democracy to select its representatives. Elections are one way. Random selection – sortition – is another." However, it should be pointed out that the ancient Greeks never used elections to select politicians, such as members of parliament; they used instead sortition, not elections, and only for one term—for obvious reasons!

By using the process of sortition to select all political officials from a group of volunteers, the aim of the Athenians was also to uphold at the same time the axiomatic principle of political equality for all those wishing to serve in a specific role, e.g. as parliamentarians. Are the theorists of democracy and the Harvard professor not aware that the renewal of a politician's term is linked to several forms of corruption and collusion? More than 3.5 billion dollars, deriving from private sources, are spent during the electoral campaigns in order to 'sell' democracy. Don't they also know that the election of politicians violates the principle of equality among those citizens wishing to become parliamentarians? If so, then how, and on what basis, do they equate democracy with the Roman republic, where the political officials were elected, and could retain their candidature for as many terms as they wished? The theorists of democracy did not invent democracy, the Athenians did, thousands of years ago; they defined the term democracy in a very specific way, and modern theorists have no right to change that definition. **Only the axiomatic principles of democracy, and the tool of sortition, used in order to select political officials for one term only, are the factors that define the system of democracy**. The citizens' assembly, where elections for single-term specialists and votes for laws and different decrees were held, was not a tool for the election of politicians. The citizens' assembly as a political tool was not capable of satisfying all the axiomatic principles of democracy. The intentions of those who had invented it were sound, but good intentions are not enough. What is more, this tool was also opening the door for collusion and corruption to pervert the course of the deliberations. Therefore, either the theorists of democracy have misunderstood what the ancient Athenians did, or they felt obliged to corrupt the original meaning of democracy in order to serve the oligarchic establishments. **The Roman system, called republic, before it evolved into imperial Rome, used elections for selecting politicians. It therefore does not qualify to step up to the rostrum of democracies. Democracy does not elect politicians, it elects only specialists for a single term only, and they are under the control of the parliament, whose members are selected by sortition!** The professor should have delved more deeply into the history of democracy, and not leave it to the theorists of democracy. **The theorists of democracy did not only serve their masters, they also discredited the system of democracy by putting it in a sack together with the rotten apples of capitalism.**

What is interesting in all of this, is that the Harvard professor together with millions of others, specialists or not, have fallen victims to the dirty games that the theorists of democracy had played in the past and still do. The professor confesses that he does not believe in the "simple" (direct?) "democracy," meaning, I assume, the one practiced by the ancient Athenians. As mentioned earlier, the ancient Athenian democracy was a hybrid type of democracy. On the one hand, it was a direct democracy for the poor for 30 to 40 days of the year, as regards the social and geographical demographics of those who participated in the deliberation of the assembly. This was true also from the point of view that, unlike the current state of affairs at the US Congress and at parliaments worldwide, where corruption and collusion are rife, this instrument only allowed for a restricted degree of collusion and corruption to interfere with its functions, because of the rules governing its deliberations, and because of the presence of all members of parliament and of most of the sworn jurists taking part in them, who were selected by sortition. On the other hand, the democracy of ancient Athens functioned as a very effective representative democracy for the rest of the year. If we compare the two systems of modern and ancient democracy, the difference is clear: in the case of the latter, when the role of the participants in the Assembly was to vote for a specialist or for a law, and not for a politician, the assembly members had the opportunity to first listen directly to the various speakers they knew well before deciding for or against their proposals, whereas in the Congress, or at the various parliaments that operate today, no one, whether inside or outside those bodies, can actually know whose voice it is that they are listening to.

Judging from the professor's writings, he must be a proponent of institutions that follow the model of representation, such as parliaments. The question he is raising, moreover, is the following: "If the many can't be relied upon, then can we craft a representative few who can?" The answer to his desperate plea is that, if he remains loyal to the system of the republic, which he mistakenly believes to be a democracy, there is no way that this can be accomplished! He and everyone else must therefore make a choice. They cannot both have their pie and eat it. After all, what brought us to this mess was precisely this republican system of government. Trying to change our world by using the same system and tools that are responsible for its failings, will not get him very far.

But that is only the least of damage caused. What is even more harmful, is that people with influence, such as professors and specialists, promote without realizing it the travesty of the concept of democracy, something which makes desperate people turn towards extremists and populists, such as Trump.

Unfortunately, the obsession today of even very educated people with the current systems of government around the world that are called democracies is so strong, that it creates for true democracy the imminent danger of being discredited, because of the undemocratic results so far produced by these so-called democracies. As a result, many citizens around the word have second thoughts about the value of democracy. One reason some American people voted for President Donald Trump was to elect a man off the beaten track, an outsider who did not belong to the establishment, which many people abhor. One can also already see the rise of the far-right extremists in Germany and France, who are longing for the "good old times" of Mussolini and Hitler. Many people faced with the results produced by these so-called democracies begin to lose faith in democracy, and this is not good progress at all.

It is therefore very important that professors especially should be clear about this, and with them most specialists, whose words have the power to penetrate into the minds of the public: we do not have here a case where an insect, one fine day, landed on a healthy apple and injected its eggs, whereby with time the apple became rotten. The system was fashioned from the beginning to contain intrinsic worms, and therefore it produces the results we are experiencing today. If we assume that we had democracy in the past, and that now we suddenly don't, we won't be able to get out of this vicious circle, because the formula for correcting the problem will not be the right one. As has been said, conducting the same experiment and expecting different results is not very wise.

Having said so much by way of introduction, let us examine one by one the symptoms (named flaws in his book) presented by Professor Lessing.

1. **They don't represent us**. By that the professor means that the congressmen, and perhaps some additional institutional structures, **do not represent the American people**. He begins Chapter I with the phrase: "The framers of our constitution gave us a 'republic.'" By that term, they meant not a simple democracy, but a 'representative democracy.' By simple democracy the Professor means the so-called direct democracy chosen by the ancient Athenians as the instrument of government, namely the citizens' assembly, to serve the principles

of democracy. We have already spoken about this and shown that it is not an appropriate tool for democracy. Here the professor calls **the republic a representative democracy**. One cannot disagree with this, but the question is what quality of representation can be achieved by that system? So far, even the professor is not happy with it, at all. The republican system of government was an invention of the Romans, and they used it for quite a while until it evolved into imperial Rome, just as the American republic turned into an imperial America. According to Aristotle's definition, a republic is not a democratic system of government, it is an oligarchic system, and, judging from the results produced by the American republic, Aristotle's definition is more than just correct. The professor was therefore carried away by the framers' declarations, whose intentions were good. He is rejecting Aristotle's definition, which was based on facts, endorsing instead the one advanced by the theorists of democracy, where they conclude that "there are two very different ways for a democracy to select its representatives. Elections are one way. Random selection – or sortition – is another"! Of course, he is not alone in this. Most people make this mistake, some deliberately, perhaps to serve a private interest. Judging from the fact that he calls the USA a democracy, when in fact the USA is a republic, one is tempted to regard the professor as someone who belongs in the former of the two groups. However, the professor, as will be explained later, belongs to the latter category.

The professor, to explain the role of sortition, writes it "presents a solution to an obvious problem," namely that democracy, wherever it was applied, "needed humans to exercise judgment." "Each case," where democracy was the system of government, "wanted to select humans who were, in a critical sense, disinterested. Each had an obvious intuition that a random selection would avoid selecting people who had the wrong reason to serve. Service would not be self-interested. Service would be service. Election could not promise the same result. People who run have an interest in running. Sometimes that interest is public regard, but not always. And the fear of those who fear elections is that the few who would choose to run are precisely the people we don't want making the decisions."

It is obvious that the professor understands clearly the purpose of using sortition in a democratic system for selecting politicians. The democratic model does not want to place in positions of power politicians who have been selected by a system that produces collusion and corruption. It is that simple. The fact that the professor is a fervent supporter of elections does not mean that he is not bothered by the production, through election, of collusion and corruption. The reason for his fervent support of elections is to be sought elsewhere. We will come back to this after we have highlighted certain other issues.

The professor and the theorists of democracy are aware of Aristotle's definition, as well as of the position of Montesquieu, who agreed with it: selection of politicians by lot relates to democracy and selection by voting relates to aristocracy. The reason for that?

Here is the professor's own explanation: "… when at the end of the eighteenth century, the two great experiments with large – scale democracy were launched – one in France and one in America – neither embraced sortition for selecting representatives. Instead, both embedded elections at their core. Theorists of democracy thus quickly (!) forgot that for hundreds of years, democratic systems had followed a different way. Very soon, the assumption was that elections are the sine qua non of democracy." As is evident, this was not a random act by those in France and America. They had to christen an oligarchic system with the name of democracy in order to satisfy both the establishment and the common people of their times. After all Benjamin Franklin, when he came out of the meeting that would decide America's constitution, said—in reply to the question "What do we have, a republic or a monarchy?"— "A republic if you can keep it"! He did not say, "You have a democracy." It was the theorists of "democracy," namely, the toadies of their masters, who said it was a democracy. Sadly, the professor, has chosen to follow these latter, even though he knows that this is not what had originally been said. I assume that one reason he does this is that he does not want to appear to be against the decisions made by the American framers. This is what he says, in his own words: "Yet it had not always been so. As Van Rebrick (16) describes, and as Oliver Dowlen (17) explains as well in his wonderful pamphlet, *Sorted: Civil Lotteries and the Future of Public Participation*, there are many examples – from ancient Greece to much of the history of Florence [author's note: which initiated the period of the Renaissance] – of governments that were filled with people who (were) selected randomly. The Greeks invented a device that would do the random selection. Their commitment to sortition survived for more than two hundred years. A Venetian lottery system survived for more than five hundred years. And even in Britten, the town of Great Yarmouth had a scheme that lasted for more than three hundred years, until it was replaced in 1835."

Finally, the professor expounds on the reason why he himself prefers the republican system, despite its inherent risk of giving rise to collusion and corruption, when elections are used to elect politicians. Again, this is what he says: "I rehearse Van Reybrouck's arguments here (p. 188) not to argue that we should eliminate elections and choose representatives by random selection. Instead, the point of the story is to drive home a point that is too often lost: that we have forever delegated to subsets of 'us' the power of government, and that such delegation has very often been a very good thing. It would be insane to require all of 'us' to 'sit' on every jury. 'We' in these cases never means 'all of us.' 'We' in these cases only ever means some of us. And the critical question that we should always be able to ask is not 'why some,' but 'why this method of selecting some.'" The professor does not give a convincing answer to this question of his, for the argument that France and the USA chose the republican system over the democratic does not hold water.

Things start to become clear now. We know that the professor does not like direct democracy. Based on this, one may conclude that he thinks that what was practiced in ancient Greece was hands-on, direct democracy. And he is not alone in this. However, as regards parliament, the ancient Athenian system was a representative democratic system. I should remind the reader that the axiomatic principles of democracy in ancient Greece were served (or were supposed to be served) by three instruments: the parliament, where the parliamentarians were selected by sortition, the citizens' assembly, where every male citizen over the age of twenty was able to participate, and the judiciary system, where the sworn jurists were selected also by sortition. In the USA we have the House of the representatives, where the representatives are elected, the Senate, where the senators are also elected, and the judiciary system, where the judges at the highest court are selected by the president, and must be approved by the Senate. The two cases have, in name at least, roughly similar institutions, but they are staffed by quite different methods. Therefore, the former is called a democracy, and the latter a republic. The Athenian parliament, as a representative institution, where all parliamentarians were selected from a group of volunteers by sortition, succeeded in protecting the citizens' assembly on several occasions from taking the wrong decisions. The latter is an instrument which failed to serve democracy's axiomatic principles in the way the inventors had initially thought it would, and for this reason any such instruments must be abandoned. One must ask therefore, and in this regard, how functional and democratic an institution the USA Senate really is? The professor is not very keen on it, and he is certainly right in this. Hence, as to the question of which is the better way to select those who represent us, history provides us with an unambiguous answer: sortition is the right way of selecting politicians, and for a single term only, not the elections and reelections of politicians.

As was mentioned earlier, we are under no constraint today to copy blindly the ancient practices as regards random selection. Today, we can refine the criteria used to acquire a group of volunteers who are willing to serve, a point that has already been developed earlier. The professor explains this himself. As he says, "… the key is to recognize how sortition was deployed to compensate for both potential weaknesses. A properly sorted public could be both representative and informed. And the lesson of history is that we should consider whether and where a sorted public might be better than an electing public – both to ensure better judgments and ensure a more representative mix" (188)! Initially, one can even allow for half of those who represent us to have the chance to be candidates for a second term, using again the method of sortition, so as to ensure some continuity in the day-to-day operations of the institution. The important thing is not to lose sight of the fact that sortition is the method that guarantees the removal of collusion and corruption from the system. In this way, we ensure that the creation of institutions, where voting is carried out, is free of the evils of modern structures of representation, and we also similarly decrease, among other things, the importance of the role played by the media today. Finally, the process is very economical because it will certainly not cost the people more than 3.5 billion dollars every time we select the political officials.

It is clear that, on the basis of all the historical evidence stated above as regards the selection of politicians by sortition, which was the principal tool that contributed to the normal functioning of democracy (i.e. by satisfying the latter's axiomatic principles), it follows that the theorists of "democracy" are obscuring historical truth for reasons that have to do with the aims of the elites in each specific period. Their main concern was (and is) to be able to exert control, through their presence in positions of power, and thus to protect the interests of the ruling class. The republican system of government was the best option for allowing the capitalistic model of production to dominate. This system in fact succeeded in killing two birds with one stone: namely, the capitalists would be able to continue enjoying their profits, and the people would be able to live, so to speak, and thanks to their revolutions, under the state of a republican, namely, a capitalistic "democracy."

The US system of government has been, from its inception, a genuinely oligarchic system (government by the few), and this is the reason why the people are not represented, as the professor admits anyway, by virtue of the proposals he is making to reinstitute democracy.

What happened is that the framers, after declaring the principles of democracy, then proceeded to invent some ad hoc political instruments to serve the democratic ideals, and this is where they stumbled, just as the ancient Greeks stumbled. However, the ancient Greeks did not stumble as badly as the framers in the US did, for the ancient Athenians never elected politicians; they selected them by sortition (by lot), as has already been mentioned, and for one term only, in order to eradicate any collusion and corruption in the system. Then, alas, they brought them back, by using as their instrument for serving the principles of democracy the so-called citizens' assembly. But even so, the ancient Athenians did much better than the framers in the US, precisely because they never elected politicians. The ancient parliament consisted of 500 single-term parliamentarians, 50 from each tribe (and all tribes had equal numbers of population, in order to warrant the principle of proportional representation). These parliamentarians were selected by sortition, and for one term only, and not through election. This method often functioned as a safety valve, preventing the citizens' assembly from taking the wrong decisions, and thus protecting to a certain extent the standards of Athenian democracy.

As has been mentioned earlier, the citizens' assembly was in session for approximately 35 to 40 days per year. The rest of the time parliament was in charge. This is something that the House of Representatives does not, whose members are, presumably, elected by the "will" of the people, and which the Professor presents as a monument to proportional representation. At least this is what the professor admits in his own writings. Indeed, how in the world is it possible for someone to call a system of single-seat electoral districts, where the winner takes all, a system of proportional representation, especially in our days, when not even 50% of those eligible to vote even take the trouble to go to the polls? What kind of representation of the people is that?

This paradox happens because the framers (the founding fathers) and the professor consider **what is merely an instrument** (a tool), chosen to serve, as they claim, the axiomatic principles of democracy, as being equivalent to these principles, without supporting their position with historical evidence that would show whether this tool does exactly what it was designated to do. They are doing precisely what the Romans did. As has been said earlier, the axiomatic principles of democracy are universal truths; tools are not, and therefore they must be changed in both form and content if they do not fulfill their purpose. The professor does in fact present the history of changes, and the different proposals made for changes to this political instrument. Let it be reminded that in ancient Greece the "will" of the people was swayed in the citizens' assembly by the persuasive ability of great orators, not elected politicians. These were ordinary citizens, not public officials, and, according to the rules of deliberation in the citizens' assembly, they could take the floor and speak on any subject on equal terms as regards time. The "will" of the people today is consistently being manipulated by the professional politicians and, of course, by the persuasive power of very strong centers of influence, which the Professor also does not fail to mention. The citizens' assembly, just as the free market of Adam Smith, would have worked perfectly provided the participants were of the same type (of equal strength).

2.  The professor tells us that **"In America, everyone gets an equal vote, regardless of the taxes that she or he pays."** What this phrase means is that, by law, every citizen has the same rights as any other, and this is indeed in line with one of the principles of democracy. It does not, however, transform a political instrument (the vote) into a principle of democracy, as the Professor claims, and this without any hesitation. What is curious here, is that, while the Professor describes the evolution of the voting process, he fails to realize that voting was not recognized as a principle, and this is why not everybody had the right to vote in earlier times, wherever voting took place. This is what happens when an axiomatic principle is substituted by a tool, which, by the way, was selected in the first place to serve the requirements of the principles of democracy.

One must examine every political instrument for the purpose of getting an answer to the following question: does the instrument serve the specific principle of democracy for which it was selected? In this case the equal rights principle means that, wherever voting takes place, every citizen has the right to vote, and their vote is equal to that of any other voter. In ancient Athens they did not exclude voting. The passing of laws, the selection of specialists, such as the generals or others, was carried out through voting in the citizens' assembly, where they assumed that all voters were free of any collusion. In fact, many **were** free of collusion, such as the 500 members of parliament, and all the six thousand sworn jurists who were able to attend (i.e. those who were not involved in a court case). These were selected by sortition and for a single term only. The only voters there, therefore, who could not be free of collusion, were those who were susceptible to bribing. This could happen in cases where decisions in the citizens' assembly were approved by a very marginal majority. In all other cases bribing could turn out to be too expensive for the bribe-giver. However, they never elected politicians, not even for one term, which is the usual practice today in our so-called democracies and, alas, for repeated terms. In ancient Athenian democracy the citizens did not want to have professional politicians, for obvious reasons. That is why they elected all the specialists needed for every sector of government activity, and for a single term only, except in the case of the generals whose term could be renewed by vote in the citizens' assembly.

Furthermore, all specialists were under the strict control of parliament, which was truly representative of the people, something Congress is not. All the above means that just because voting takes place, it does not also follow that we have democracy. You have democracy where the equal rights principle holds true. Today, as most of us know, voting does not express the "will" of the people, and it does not lead to democracy. However, it costs a lot of money to the taxpayers. For even if it may appear that the funding of political parties and party candidates comes from private donations, in reality this is not so. It all comes from the taxpayer's pocket.

3. **It is generally said that one evil is followed by many others.** The professor, a staunch supporter of voting, which he also calls arbitrarily a principle of democracy, analyzes in his book the effects of gerrymandering (partisan manipulation of the boundaries of an electoral

district in such a way as to ensure the reelection of their candidate). This kind of unethical practice, which is a bipartisan "achievement," is basically a consequence of the implementation of the instrument called voting. The republican system of governing is, supposedly, used to ensure democratic representation; instead, one gets the people's representation of the type that gerrymandering produces. According to the professor's own data, almost 85% of the seats in the House of Representatives are made safe for the incumbent congressman, or the party's candidate, through gerrymandering, and no election whatsoever can change that!

The political instrument of voting, combined with an electoral law that recognizes only single-seat electoral districts, effectively destroys the representation of the people. This is the reason why in the USA there are only two parties, the Republican and the Democratic Party, which can win seats in Congress. The same holds true for state elections. Under such conditions, the representation of the people in Congress is dictated by the two parties and not by the people. Here the case is worse than in the case of gerrymandering in the electoral districts, which provides, as Professor Lessing elegantly describes it, a way "for politicians to pick the voters rather than the voters picking politicians." Here the two parties don't just pick voters, they force voters to pick between just two options! Such features can be seen only in very autarchic political systems. Even Erdogan, the president of the Turkish Republic, does better on this score than the USA does. In order to prevent the election of Kurds into parliament, Erdogan uses an electoral law which requires that a party gets at least 10% of the votes in order to elect parliamentarians. Nonetheless, the electoral law does allow more than two parties to pass the lower threshold of votes and enter parliament, which is something the US electoral law does not allow for.

One-seat electoral districts, where the winner takes all, combined with the way that funding is carried out, and the strategy of gerrymandering, make the US democracy a farce. These kinds of tools have no connection whatsoever with a representational democracy. This regime is more like an autarchy that has always the same two partners in power. **And here, we have Trump worrying about the leftists seizing power!**

The American political system is a fortress that cannot be easily conquered, unless the partners in power decide to dissociate themselves from it, and this should be the target of those who fight for democracy, whom Trump calls leftists. US "democracy" is the hardest case of all the so-called "democracies" as a candidate for the future club of real democracies.

As far as the Senate is concerned, things there are even worse, and I agree with the proposal made by some for its abolition. Professor Lessing (15, page 31) describes the case of the Senate as follows: "Over time the nation learned that the framers' design for the Senate was fraught. Vesting the appointment of senators in state legislators was an open invitation to corruption. A legislator as a collective could not be held responsible for a bad or corrupt senator, but individual legislators could benefit enormously from selling Senate seats to the highest bidders. By the end of the nineteenth century, the institution had become a complete embarrassment."

Professor Lessing makes a special mention of the case of "Senator" W. A. Clark, a local industrialist from Montana who, in 1899, bought his seat for the Senate by paying, according to his own admission, $272,000 (about $8 million in current value). This demonstrates that the system was fraught from the start.

4.  Other evils introduced into the system are caused by the same underlying source, namely the process of voting. The most catastrophic for democracy among these is the central credo of a fundraising campaign, which ensures a total sellout of democracy. Something like 3 billion dollars is the average amount spent during the last elections for legislators in the USA. In the recent presidential election (2020), the amount spent surpassed all previous similar expenditures by more than 500 million dollars. This money is spent not to elect the best, but those most useful to the strong centers of influence, and no matter what may be proposed to harness this Lernaean Hydra, it will not be successful. The professor does make a proposal for the funding of elections to be through public money, with which I totally agree, but, as he also explains, the Republican Party does not agree with this idea, since Republican money would then be used to support Democratic candidates! Fewer than 25% of those eligible to vote represent the Republican Party's total number of voters, and yet a healthy and extremely economical measure for the people is being blocked—and this is considered democratic. I would say that the framers framed, air tight, the people of the USA, and what will most probably happen

to them in the future is that they will fall flat on their faces, something worse than the shackles they now have around their necks. Trump already leads the way, and he is not alone.

The professor is obsessed with the idea that democracy cannot exist without a process to elect politicians, even though he admits that "elections are rarely anything but flawed and multiplying the number of offices subject to election is rarely anything but corruption." Nevertheless, when it comes to "an office that must, by its nature, be elected – such as the office of a representative or a president – then humility should guide us to complement the process with guidance from an "us" that we all should respect" (15, p. 194). When things go wrong, as they did in the case of Donald Trump, then those to blame are the people, and not the voting process which is, usually, and indirectly, well under control by strong centers of influence. The same thing is true about abstention from voting. They don't blame the system, namely voting, they blame the absentees! His response to this type of control seems to be the addition of "a layer of citizen advice into the process to help guide the ultimate results." He seems to forget that the institutions of representation already have, not one but several layers of "citizen" advice integrated into the process, consisting of those who fund their campaign for election or reelection. The politicians exhibit, and openly in fact, their preferences, which are not the type of 'citizen advice' layer suggested by the professor. In order to be able to add this layer of citizen advice into the process to help guide the ultimate results, one needs to have truly representative institutions, and this cannot come about through the election of politicians, namely congressmen or parliamentarians. If the professor's prophecy that "elections are going to be with us forever," as they "should be," according to him (15, p. 192), comes to be true, then his plea that "They don't represent us" will never succeed in reclaiming his democracy. In my own proposal, elections for certain cases are envisaged, and they are in line with true democracy, as it is explained in the next chapter.

In selecting politicians by a voting process, the only thing we accomplish is to add more and more obstacles to the struggle to reclaim democracy. For example, the professor states that "we do not have the institutions to ensure we know enough to choose well." With this he means the institutions related to the media, which provide the information to the public. He states further that "if democracy is going to survive, it will not survive through a reliance on these forms of media alone," neglecting to say that the problem is not the media, but the way the political parties operate.

The professor is not the only one who does not have a good opinion of the role of the media. Many people blame the press and the different TV news channels for many of the ills we have enumerated above. It is true that these sources of information, which report and produce news, do contribute, to a very high degree, to the shaping of public opinion. And it is true that not all of them contribute, in a positive way, to sound news reporting. But who gives them the opportunity, in the first place, to do what they are doing? Isn't it the political parties themselves that invite the development and growth of such centers of information? Aren't the political parties' needs to win rather than lose votes, and their candidates' need to secure or renew their term in office, combined with the way elections are funded, that create the incentives for investments in this area by those who have the ability to do so, and by means of which those who own this sector tie with chains all these political officials and, along with them, Democracy? This, and not the media, is the reason why democracy is facing the danger of not surviving. Political parties, by accepting the tool of voting to serve democracy, effectively ruin the prospects of a democratic way of governing to prosper.

## Some useful ideas once democracy is reclaimed

The professor's commitment to holding elections for selecting congressmen, and his proposal for holding shadow conventions, are two ideas that contradict each other. Why so? Because the results of the shadow convention may be of the type that will obligate Congress to decide for or against them. For why would the Congress vote a law that may restrict its present authority? What if the shadow convention decides that from now on the congressmen will be selected by sortition and for a single term only, with no option for reelection? (And, by the way, this is why sortition in selecting the participants to the convention is fine and dandy). I consider the shadow convention an excellent idea which should be implemented once democracy is reclaimed. Until then, the case is like that where one puts the cart before the horse. Gun control policies are a vivid example. The overwhelming majority is in favor of gun control, so why is it that Congress is continuously dragging its feet? Let us not have any illusions. The only thing these ideas can accomplish, especially those on which people are actively working, is to educate more and more people to the point of realizing that meaningful changes must be made. Elected and reelected politicians go hand and hand with collusion, and at times with corruption. Instead of wasting valuable time working on ideas relating to actual changes which, however, need the approval of Congress, where neither the politicians nor the lobbyists will allow them to pass, it is logical that activists should think at the same time about getting engaged with issues which can be promoted with success. Such issues are those that do not need the approval of Congress, and the creation of new political parties of the type I propose, is one such way of successful engagement.

### 2.6 Registered Abstention from Voting is High. Why?

In previous sections we had the opportunity to demonstrate how the process of voting for politicians leads to the production of collusion and corruption. And we also said that the abstention of eligible voters from the voting process has to do with the negative consequences of voting, which render this instrument inappropriate for serving democracy. In this section we will present the results from studies carried out all over the world by researchers, institutes, government and non-governmental organizations, as well as university professors, for the purpose of demonstrating the connection between negative voting results and the high abstention of eligible voters from voting.

As we will see, all the studies on the causes of abstention from votes for politicians report that with time a continuous decrease of participation of eligible voters in general elections is observed. The abstention from voting has increased steadily, and has reached levels of 50% or higher among those eligible to vote. High percentages of participation to voting is only seen to be taking place in countries where dictatorships are in power. As a result, political parties see that they are running out of raw material, which is equivalent to running out of business! After all, in the words of Mary Scott (18), a researcher for Catch 21 – a charitable organization in the UK – and commenting on high abstention, especially, among young people, "youth is the future of voters, commentators and politicians. What young person today thinks politics are important?"

*The findings of these investigations tell us that there* is more than one reason why this is happening, but I would say that, in essence, it appears that almost all of them are connected to an important factor: More and more citizens stopped believing that anything can be change by their voting!

The United Kingdom's Electoral Commission notes in its 2002 report, ***Voter engagement and young people (19)***, that the reasons behind young people's abstention from voting have to do with " disillusion (the view that it makes no difference who wins), apathy (the lack of interest in politics), impact (the view that an individual vote won't make a difference), alienation (the view that politics is not for young people), knowledge (not knowing enough about politics to cast a vote) and inconvenience (voting is too time consuming)."

In 2002 the **UK Electoral Commission** also notes that "the problem of falling turnout is not exclusively British. Turnout seems to be falling in most established democracies across all orders of election (20, 21) and crucially for our study it appears to be falling most swiftly among the youngest sections of the electorate (22, 23). In the study of voting across many (mostly European) countries Franklin relates turnout to several individual-level features. He finds that the best single fixed predictor of turnout in European Parliament elections was age, with the youngest sections of the electorate being the most likely to opt out of voting (24 p.220). In a study of nine democratic countries in the late 1990s Blasi reports that 'the two most crucial socio-economic determinants of voting are education and age" (25 p. 25).

The findings of the **Market and Opinion Research International** (MORI) 2001 (26) report show that "young people were the most likely to say that "no one party stands for me" and to claim that they felt 'powerless' in the electoral process. The parties were not perceived as very distinct from each other, thus reducing the incentive to vote." Commenting on a survey commissioned by the **Carnegie Young People's Initiative**, Ravi Gurumurthy, its chairperson, recognized that "young people want to be involved but they feel that the present political structure does not allow them sufficient opportunity" (27).

Data from **the British Social Attitude Survey (28)** suggest that only one in ten of 18–25-year-olds were very interested or just interested in politics. According to the MORI data, young voters were less likely to claim to have voted through a sense of civic duty than the rest of the electorate. Young non-voters were the most likely to complain that 'no one party stands for me' or that they felt 'powerless' in the electoral process.

The UK Electoral Commission's 2002 report notes that "Politicians are widely seen as unrepresentative of the wider population in the UK in terms of age, gender, ethnicity and social class. Only one in every eight MPs is a woman (there were 118 female MPs in 2001); only 12 MPs are from black and minority ethnic communities, and all of these represent the Labor Party. In terms of age, the established career structure of politics effectively rules out large-scale representation by young people. After the 2001 general election only five of the 659 MPs in the Commons were under 30, and the average age of MPs was 49 (29 p.199)."

Corresponding findings in the USA, as reported in the UK Electoral Commission's 2002 Report, run along the same tracks, reporting low turnout rates among first-time voters in the 1996 US presidential election, and claiming that young people were becoming "increasingly alienated from the political process" (30, 31). It further comments on the 'hatred' for politics exhibited by the American youth, whereas Nye (1997) (32) asserted that young electors were the most likely to have a deep distrust of government and government structures. Eliasoph (1998) (33) identified a phenomenon she termed the 'shrinking circle of concern,' as Americans increasingly attempt to 'avoid politics' in everyday life as well as in electoral contests.

The **International Institute for Democracy and Electoral Assistance (International IDEA)**, of Sweden in its 1999 (34) report zeroes in on the electoral abstention which they characterize as a problem of democracy. In their foreword they write: "For all of us who believe that democracy is the most effective political system for the common good and for achieving a balance between the authority necessary in all human societies and the freedom of the people – or the "least evil," according to Churchill's famous definition – the phenomenon of low or limited citizens' participation in elections, especially among youth, observed in many democratic countries today, cannot but be a matter of concern. It is obvious that the strength of a government and its subsequent capacity or power to carry out its functions and do whatever is necessary to realize the common good largely rests on the degree of support it has among the population throughout the country. It is precisely this support that is expressed by democratic electoral processes. For this reason, the phenomenon of electoral abstention, which appears to be increasing in many democratic societies today, awakens justified concern and deserves to be examined in order to discover the causes and find ways to rectify it. It is even more important when this non-participation in elections occurs mainly among the young, as is the case in various countries."

The International IDEA published a report that analyzed statistics from more than 1,400 parliamentary and presidential elections held between 1945 and 1997 in over 170 countries. Among the findings of the report is that turnout across the globe rose steadily between 1945 and 1990, increasing from 61% in the 1940s to 68% in the 1980s. Since 1990, however, the average has decreased to 64%. (Survey Data Sources and Characteristics: see International IDEA report, page 22, Table 1) (34)

**On the basis of these statistics should we assume that new wars are coming in order to set people back on track?**

According to The International IDEA, in a comparative perspective, the turnout level for young citizens is particularly low in countries where the overall turnout level is also relatively low: Switzerland (50.2%), France (63.2%), Portugal (63.7%), Ireland (64.1%), Finland (68.6%), and Norway (75.9%). Spain and Great Britain show participation rates for electors between 18 and 29 years that are very close to the overall West European mean of 80.9%. (West) Germany, Denmark, The Netherlands, Greece and Sweden show levels of turnout between 85 and 90%, while in Belgium and Italy the turnout for this age group is over 95%. The higher the country's average level of turnout, the higher the level of participation by young citizens. Only the case of Ireland stands out as an exception. While the overall level of turnout in this country is like that in Great Britain or Spain, the turnout rate of young citizens is much lower (64.1% as compared to over 80% in Spain or Great Britain).

The conclusion of the institute, which is included in its report, namely that: "the higher the country's average level of turnout, the higher the level of participation by young citizens," is not very impressive. Yet what did the researchers expect would happen? In a politically engaged family, where the parents consciously abstain from voting, for all the reasons already mentioned above, these same parents talk with their children about the political conditions in their country, and not only in their country. They tell them that the situation cannot be changed by holding on to the instrument of voting, which is responsible, in the first place, for this whole mess. If, at some point, the parents go to vote it is because they want to delay worse things from happening (as in the case of Donald Trump), hoping for a miracle to happen. Don't the researchers know the saying "like father like son"? That is exactly what is happening, which is why we see the number of absentees growing.

"Because of the unique role of elections in a democratic system, voting also has a special place among the many different forms of political participation that citizens can engage in to influence government. Furthermore, voting is the only form of participation in which each citizen has an equal say (one person, one vote). The right to vote is a great equalizer in political influence; in practice, however, this is only true for those who exercise it." If this were the case, there would be no problems for democracy, even with abstention, because what matters here most is to know who forms the "will" of the people. By now, many will know who forms the "will" of the people, and this is the reason why these oligarchical systems of government are facing problems. The bell tolls for them, judging from the increase in the political power of the extreme right across Western cultures.

"If those who vote differ significantly in key political attributes from those who do not vote, a distortion in representation is likely to ensue. After all, the outcome of an election only reflects the judgment of the voting public. Groups known to have a lower turnout rate may be neglected in policymaking and thus in policy outcomes. Universal participation in elections ensures the faithful representation of the popular will and thus prevents such distortions. It also enhances the legitimacy of the system. By performing their role as voters, citizens affirm their support for the political order. This promotes political stability, but it is also inherently desirable on normative grounds. According to democratic theory, the right to vote in elections should not only be universally guaranteed, it should also be exercised. **The reality of contemporary elections, however, reveals that there has been a decline in voter turnout throughout the world."** This means that what preceded this last sentence apparently had to do with some wonderland, such as those we have seen lately in movies.

And the report continues: "If young people fail to acquire habits of good citizenship and democratic responsibility in their formative years, the future of democracy may be in question. By voting, young people have the same ability as others to exercise political influence or pressure." Such attributes cannot be developed by young people under oligarchical systems of government. However, they are very much needed in a truly democratic state, and it is in such a state that such ethical and civic qualities can be acquired by the younger generation.

**"Political integration strengthens democracy:** Young people who are involved in the electoral process affirm their support for democracy as well as acquiring a stake in the system and an appreciation that they, too, can affect politics and policy. Indeed, political integration of youth may promote public order and democratic stability if young people are given a real voice, their vote is seen as meaningful and influential, and the system is responsive to their input.

Ample research has established that turnout is affected by many factors. Some of them relate to the individual (such as age, level of social integration, interest in politics or attachment to a party). Others relate to the political context where elections take place (the presence or absence of compulsory voting, the type of electoral system, the characteristics of the party system and the election). All these factors affect turnout, and at the same time they are interrelated, making it difficult to estimate their relative effects on the level of electoral participation. The data presented here should be considered an exploratory analysis of the effect of these variables on youth turnout. In order to reach more definitive conclusions, further multivariate analyses should be performed." The sermon to the young is over, and the researchers now come face to face with their findings as these reflect real life. They are as follows:

"The most important reasons, which young people invoke for not voting," according to the report of the International IDEA, are:

- *Disillusionment about the political system;*
- *Complaints about the political parties and candidates;*
- *Parties being unresponsive to their needs, lack of information about candidates;*
- *Not interested in the political and/or electoral process;*
- *Doubts about the effectiveness or the difference their vote would make;*
- *Complaints about corruption in politics;*

To sum up, the conclusion **of young people is one of disillusionment with the political system, political parties and candidates."** This conclusion does not describe a democratic system of government, and it ought to have made the researchers think again.

**For the USA,** the reasons given by the International IDEA report as to why young people do not vote, are not significantly different from those given by older non-voters. Expressions of concern about the health of American democracy are increasingly being heard. Voter turnout in the 1996 presidential election was 49%, the lowest level since 1924. Off-year, or mid-term elections draw less voter attention and interest, and turnouts for these elections since the 1970s have ranged between 37% and 40%. Despite last minute, million-dollar "get out and vote" blitzes on election day, the November 1998 election (where no presidential contest was taking place) involved only 38% of the eligible adult electorate (about the same level as the 1990 and 1994 elections).

The problem of electoral non-participation is especially acute among the young. Since the endorsement of the Twenty-Sixth Amendment to the American Constitution in 1971, all citizens over the age of 18 have the right to vote in elections at any level in the country. However, voter turnout for the youngest group of eligible voters, the 18- to 24-year-olds, is the lowest of any age group. Only 42.8% of this age group claimed to have voted in the 1992 Presidential election, a figure that fell further to a 30-plus year low of 32.4% in the 1996 Presidential election (35).

It appears that for the members of this institute, the problem for democracy is the abstention from voting, and not the abstention from politics, which has very much to do with the negative progress of the common good. The problem is not linked to the future of democracy, it is linked to the future of oligarchical regimes which increasingly run the risk of being substituted by dictatorships. What is for them certain, is that Sweden has no problem with its democracy. They worry about the rest of the world.

In the French National Report (36) it is stated that "young generations are always suspected of being less interested in politics and less politicized than their elders." But this observation is not really founded. They are as interested in politics as the rest of the population. What they keep at a distance is politicians and political affairs concerning partisan quarrels and electoral competition. But they are concerned about national issues and international problems. So, their answer to this question depends on what we consider as politics.

This first overview of young French people's interest and competence in politics gives an idea of the way politics form a part of their daily life. "Politics is not outside their experience and concerns. 56% declare that their fathers are interested in politics, 47% say the same of their mothers, 27% of their best friend. They are used to getting some political news: 64% follow the news every day or several times a week. Television is the form of media used by most: 68% watch TV first, while other media lag far behind (5% use the radio, 7% the newspapers, 7% the Internet). They are more concerned by national (48%) and international (41%) aspects than by local (33%) and European (33%) ones."

Nevertheless, when they are asked about what is politics for them, the image they give of the political universe is primarily negative: "69% of young people believe that politics means empty promises, 64% think it is a game played by old men, 57% believe that politics is only about corruption, and 50% think that politics does not address their concerns. Most young people seem very disillusioned by politics. Only 38% believe it is a way to create a better world… Nevertheless, even if politics is mainly associated with negative aspects, it is also linked to conventional understanding: "party activities" and "voting" reach the highest level of consensus (69%), to describe what they understand by politics. Moreover, more than half of the sample perceives politics to solve international problems (58%), or societal conflicts (52%), and to take care of social issues (50%)."

The general conclusion of the report is that:

*"We must keep in mind three main results.*

*The first one is the importance that young people still give to voting. It is not only considered as the most effective political action but also as a symbolic link to guarantee democracy.*

*The second one is the importance of the abstention among youth, even if in our survey it appears minimized. Part of this abstention has a political signification and is used as a new democratic tool to weigh on the political system, especially among educated young people and students. Another part is more sociological and expresses less critical attitudes than distance and disinterest towards politics. This sociological non-voting is more developed among less educated youth, having already left school, and experiencing difficulties regarding their social integration within the labor market.*

*The third one concerns the growing number of protest votes, giving suffrage to extremist parties or to non-governmental parties. Gender has a real impact, and young women express more choices outside the classical partisan game. The weakness of partisan identification maintains a high level of electoral volatility and contributes to the general crisis of the political representation which is deeper among youth.*

*General attitudes towards politics are for most young people negative. And French politicians must face a strong distrust and a lack of confidence, which are particularly problematic among the uneducated young but also significant among educated ones."*

The third point, and the final general conclusion of the French report cancel out the importance of the former two points. The third point highlights a picture of the actions of all these people who consciously abstain from voting. Yes, most of them are being radicalized and veer towards the ultra-right and ultra-left. That is the result of the discreditation of democracy, by those cap-italist contractors who christen oligarchy with the name of democracy. Perhaps this may not bother them that much. After all, the production models in both camps do not differ in actual practice.

One would expect that at least one of all those researchers would think that instead of trying to convince or coerce the eligible voters to go and vote, it would be better to explore the possibility of substituting the instrument of voting with some other instrument which would, at last, serve the axiomatic principles of democracy. After all, so many voters who were asked why they did not go to vote, answered, in plain words, that they did not like the outcomes of the voting. Corruption is one of these outcomes, they said. Lack of a fair and democratic representation in the legislative institutions was another, a third the fact that no matter who is winning, there is nothing in it for them. And yet no, not one of the researchers thought of the existing need to invent other alternative ways of serving the axiomatic principles of democracy. None of them thought of going off the beaten track. This is how deeply addicted to the instrument of voting are even the many specialists in this world., The latter is, in fact, for them the main and the only characteristic feature that implies, and guarantees at the same time, just by itself, the existence of democracy, despite the catastrophic results that it produces. They did not neglect, however, to blame the voters who abstain for different but serious reasons from voting, and to hold them responsible for the problem's democracy is facing today. They did not neglect to start inventing "educational" programs for bringing the "lost" sheep back to the path of virtue. Well, what can one expect from the contractors of oligarchy?

The researchers who compiled all these reports carry on with their re-search and their study of the ways by which the abstention from voting will decrease. And regardless of what the young people say on why they don't bother to vote, the researchers recommend measures for what is in fact brain washing, or coercing of the young (!). Here are the suggested brainwashing techniques and their recommended action list:

- Promote voter registration by young people of voting age;
- Promote voting by young people of voting age;
- Educate young voters;
- Get youth to follow political news, seek information, and discuss pol-itics;

- Prepare future voters through simulations, mock elections, and civic education;
- Get teachers to assume the role of civic educators;
- Get parents to introduce their children to democracy and act as role models.

The programs suggested by the report, which aim at changing youth attitudes, are expected to accomplish one or several of the following:

- Persuade youth to value the right to vote;
- Instill civic norms, a sense of duty or citizen obligation;
- Get youth to affirm support for democracy through voting;
- Persuade youth that the vote is their choice; foster a sense that voting is a way to influence politics, and to force politicians and parties to pay attention;
- Make youth aware of their (potential) voting power as a group;
- Raise group consciousness (get young people to think of themselves as part of a political group with distinct interests, ideas and needs);
- Persuade youth to vote in order to balance or counteract the voting power of other groups.

**The reports don't forget also the motivational approach through slogans and messages.** Non-voting can be viewed as one of many challenges confronting society in its attempt to get individuals to behave in socially desirable ways. To do this, policymakers and their non-official partners may adopt several options:

- **Coercion** – require people to conform by force of law (and possible sanctions). In the case of non-voting, this option takes the form of mandatory or compulsory voting, which may not render voting enjoyable in the short term but may help establish or reinforce a social norm of participation as a citizen duty over the long term.
- **Rewards** – encourage people to vote by means of incentives or rewards, in this case, social approval and reinforcement.
- **Persuasion** – convince youth to participate of its own free "will."

These kinds of ways of trying to change the attitudes of the eligible voters and make them go to the polls and vote, might work for democracy if there is a democracy at all to begin with. The absentees, however, know that any voting in today's so-called democracies only achieves one thing, to pass the power, as is usually done, to the same few, as befits, moreover, an oligarchic establishment. The absentees know better than anybody that to go to the polls and vote, thus legalizing with their participation an oligarchic regime, is an act against, and not for democracy. Levitsky and Ziblatt (37) demonstrate in their book, *How Democracies Die,* how these oligarchical regimes can be transformed into criminal dictatorships.

The addiction of most citizens to this pseudo-democracy, which is represented exclusively by the voting tool, may not be a universal truth, yet it is certainly a universal paradox. Not even Einstein was able to bypass this trap of accepting this oligarchic invention as being a democracy: living in the USA it was not possible for him to accept the so-called American democracy, which terrified him, as a sound way of living. As a result, he too was radicalized, as many voters are today, and chose socialism as a refuge. Here is how he positions himself vis-à-vis the political front of that time in an article of his, with the title "*Why Socialism?,*" published in the first issue of the **Monthly Review** in May 1949:

"Is it advisable for one who is not an expert on economic and social issues to express views about socialism? I believe for several reasons that it is.

Let us first consider the question from the point of view of scientific knowledge. It might appear that there are no essential methodological differences between astronomy and economics: scientists in both fields attempt to discover laws of general acceptability for a circumscribed group of phenomena in order to make the interconnection of these phenomena as clearly understandable as possible. But in reality, such methodological differences do exist. The discovery of general laws in the field of economics is made difficult by the circumstance that observed economic phenomena are often affected by many factors which are very hard to evaluate separately. In addition, the experience which has accumulated since the beginning of the so-called civilized period of human history has—as is well known—been largely influenced and limited by causes which are by no means exclusively economic in nature. For example, most of the major states of history owed their existence to conquest. The conquering peoples established themselves, legally and economically, as the privileged class of the conquered country. They seized for themselves a monopoly of the land ownership and appointed a priesthood from among their own ranks. The priests, in control of education, made the class division of society into a permanent institution and created a system of values by which the people were thenceforth, to a large extent unconsciously, guided in their social behavior.

But historic tradition is, so to speak, of yesterday; nowhere have we really overcome what Thorstein Veblen called "the predatory phase" of human development. The observable economic facts belong to that phase and even such laws as we can derive from them are not applicable to other phases. Since the real purpose of socialism is precisely to overcome and advance beyond the predatory phase of human development, economic science in its present state can throw little light on the socialist society of the future.

Second, socialism is directed towards a social-ethical end. Science, however, cannot create ends and, even less, instill them in human beings; science, at most, can supply the means by which to attain certain ends. But the ends themselves are conceived by personalities with lofty ethical ideals and—if these ends are not stillborn, but vital and vigorous—are adopted and carried forward by those many human beings who, half unconsciously, determine the slow evolution of society.

For these reasons, we should be on our guard not to overestimate science and scientific methods when it is a question of human problems; and **we should not assume that experts are the only ones who have a right to express themselves on questions affecting the organization of society**.

Innumerable voices have been asserting for some time now that human society is passing through a crisis, that its stability has been gravely shattered. It is characteristic of such a situation that individuals feel indifferent or even hostile toward the group, small or large, to which they belong. In order to illustrate my meaning, let me record here a personal experience. I recently discussed with an intelligent and well-disposed man the threat of another war, which in my opinion would seriously endanger the existence of mankind, and I remarked that only a supra-national organization would offer protection from that danger. Thereupon my visitor, very calmly and coolly, said to me: "Why are you so deeply opposed to the disappearance of the human race?"

I am sure that as little as a century ago no one would have so lightly made a statement of this kind. It is the statement of a man who has striven in vain to attain an equilibrium within himself and has more or less lost hope of succeeding. It is the expression of a painful solitude and isolation from which so many people are suffering in these days. What is the cause? Is there a way out?

It is easy to raise such questions, but difficult to answer them with any degree of assurance. I must try, however, as best I can, although I am very conscious of the fact that our feelings and strivings are often contradictory and obscure and that they cannot be expressed in easy and simple formulas.

**Man is, at one and the same time, a solitary being and a social being.** As a solitary being, he attempts to protect his own existence and that of those who are closest to him, to satisfy his personal desires, and to develop his innate abilities. As a social being, he seeks to gain the recognition and affection of his fellow human beings, to share in their pleasures, to comfort them in their sorrows, and to improve their conditions of life. Only the existence of these varied, frequently conflicting, strivings accounts for the special character of a man, and their specific combination determines the extent to which an individual can achieve an inner equilibrium and can contribute to the well-being of society. It is quite possible that the relative strength of these two drives is, in the main, fixed by inheritance. But the personality that finally emerges is largely formed by the environment in which a man happens to find himself during his development, by the structure of the society in which he grows up, by the tradition of that society, and by its appraisal of particular types of behavior. The abstract concept "society" means to the individual human being the total of his direct and indirect relations to his contemporaries and to all the people of earlier generations. The individual is able to think, feel, strive, and work by himself; but he depends so much upon society—in his physical, intellectual, and emotional existence—that it is impossible to think of him, or to understand him, outside the framework of society. It is "society" which provides man with food, clothing, a home, the tools of work, language, the forms of thought, and most of the content of thought; his life is made possible through the labor and the accomplishments of the many millions past and present who are all hidden behind the small word "society."

It is evident, therefore, that the dependence of the individual upon society is a fact of nature which cannot be abolished—just as in the case of ants and bees.

However, while the whole life process of ants and bees is fixed down to the smallest detail by rigid, hereditary instincts, the social pattern and interrelationships of human beings are very variable and susceptible to change.

Memory, the capacity to make new combinations, the gift of oral communication has made possible developments among human being which are not dictated by biological necessities. Such developments manifest themselves in traditions, institutions, and organizations; in literature; in scientific and engineering accomplishments; in works of art. This explains how it happens that, in a certain sense, man can influence his life through his own conduct, and that in this process conscious thinking and wanting can play a part.

**Man acquires at birth, through heredity, a biological constitution which we must consider fixed and unalterable, including the natural urges which are characteristic of the human species. In addition, during his lifetime, he acquires a cultural constitution which he adopts from society through communication and through many other types of influences. It is this cultural constitution which, with the passage of time, is subject to change and which determines to a very large extent the relationship between the individual and society. Modern anthropology has taught us, through comparative investigation of so-called primitive cultures, that the social behavior of human beings may differ greatly, depending upon prevailing cultural patterns and the types of organization which predominate in society. It is on this that those who are striving to improve the lot of man may ground their hopes: human beings are not condemned, because of their biological constitution, to annihilate each other or to be at the mercy of a cruel, self-inflicted fate.**

**If we ask ourselves how the structure of society and the cultural attitude of man should be changed in order to make human life as satisfying as possible, we should constantly be conscious of the fact that there are certain conditions which we are unable to modify. As mentioned before, the biological nature of man is, for all practical purposes, not subject to change. Furthermore, technological and demographic developments of the last few centuries have created conditions which are here to stay. In relatively densely settled populations with the goods which are indispensable to their continued existence, an extreme division of labor and a highly centralized productive apparatus are necessary. The time—which, looking back, seems so idyllic—is gone forever when individuals or relatively small groups could be completely self-sufficient. It is only a slight exaggeration to say that mankind constitutes even now a planetary community of production and consumption.**

**I have now reached the point where I may indicate briefly what to me constitutes the essence of the crisis of our time. It concerns the relationship of the individual to society. The individual has become more conscious than ever of his dependence upon society. But he does not experience this dependence as a positive asset, as an organic tie, as a protective force, but rather as a threat to his natural rights, or even to his economic existence. Moreover, his position in society is such that the egotistical drives of his make-up are constantly being accentuated, while his social drives, which are by nature weaker, progressively deteriorate. All human beings, whatever their position in society, are suffering from this process of deterioration. Unknowingly prisoners of their own egotism, they feel insecure, lonely, and deprived of the naive, simple, and unsophisticated enjoyment of life. Man can find meaning in life, short and perilous as it is, only through devoting himself to society.**

The economic anarchy of capitalist society as it exists today is, in my opinion, the real source of the evil. We see before us a huge community of producers the members of which are unceasingly striving to deprive each other of the fruits of their collective labor—not by force, but overall, in faithful compliance with legally established rules. In this respect, it is important to realize that the means of production—that is to say, the entire productive capacity that is needed for producing consumer goods as well as additional capital goods—may legally be, and for the most part are, the private property of individuals.

For the sake of simplicity, in the discussion that follows I shall call "workers" all those who do not share in the ownership of the means of production—although this does not quite correspond to the customary use of the term. The owner of the means of production can purchase the labor power of the worker. By using the means of production, the worker produces new goods which become the property of the capitalist. The essential point about this process is the relation between what the worker produces and what he is paid, both measured in terms of real value. Insofar as the labor contract is "free," what the worker receives is determined not by the real value of the goods he produces, but by his minimum needs and by the capitalists' requirements for labor power in relation to the number of workers competing for jobs. It is important to understand that even in theory the payment of the worker is not determined by the value of his product.

**Private capital tends to become concentrated in few hands, partly because of competition among the capitalists, and partly because technological development and the increasing division of labor encourage the formation of larger units of production at the expense of smaller ones. The result of these developments is an oligarchy of private capital the enormous power of which cannot be effectively checked even by a democratically organized political society. This is true since the members of legislative bodies are selected by political parties, largely financed or otherwise influenced by private capitalists who, for all practical purposes, separate the electorate from the legislature. The consequence is that the representatives of the people do not in fact sufficiently protect the interests of the underprivileged sections of the population. Moreover, under existing conditions, private capitalists inevitably control, directly or indirectly, the main sources of information (press, radio, education). It is thus extremely difficult, and indeed in most cases quite impossible, for the individual citizen to come to objective conclusions and to make intelligent use of his political rights.**

The situation prevailing in an economy based on the private ownership of capital is thus characterized by two main principles: first, means of production (capital) are privately owned and the owners dispose of them as they see fit; second, the labor contract is free. Of course, there is no such thing as a pure capitalist society in this sense. It should be noted that the **workers, through long and bitter political struggles**, have succeeded in securing a somewhat improved form of the "free labor contract" for certain categories of workers. But taken as a whole, the present-day economy does not differ much from "pure" capitalism.

**Production is carried on for profit, not for use**. There is no provision that all those able and willing to work will always be able to find employment; an "army of unemployed" almost always exists. The worker is constantly in fear of losing his job. Since unemployed and poorly paid workers do not provide a profitable market, the production of consumers' goods is restricted, and great hardship is the consequence. Technological progress frequently results in more unemployment rather than in an easing of the burden of work for all. **The profit motive, in conjunction with competition among capitalists, is responsible for an instability in the accumulation and utilization of capital which leads to increasingly severe depressions. Unlimited competition**

**leads to a huge waste of labor, and to that crippling of the social consciousness of individuals which I mentioned before.**

This crippling of individuals I consider the worst evil of capitalism. Our whole educational system suffers from this evil. An exaggerated competitive attitude is inculcated into the student, who is trained to worship acquisitive success as a preparation for his future career.

I am convinced there is only one way to eliminate these grave evils, namely through the establishment of a socialist economy, accompanied by an educational system which would be oriented toward social goals. In such an economy, the means of production are owned by society itself and are utilized in a planned fashion. A planned economy, which adjusts production to the needs of the community, would distribute the work to be done among all those able to work and would guarantee a livelihood to every man, woman, and child. The education of the individual, in addition to promoting his own innate abilities, would attempt to develop in him a sense of responsibility for his fellow men in place of the glorification of power and success in our present society.

Nevertheless, it is necessary to remember that a planned economy is not yet socialism. A planned economy as such may be accompanied by the complete enslavement of the individual. The achievement of socialism requires the solution of some extremely difficult socio-political problems: how is it possible, in view of the far-reaching centralization of political and economic power, to prevent bureaucracy from becoming all-powerful and overweening? How can the rights of the individual be protected and therewith a democratic counterweight to the power of bureaucracy be assured?

**Clarity about the aims and problems of socialism is of greatest significance in our age of transition."**

At the beginning of his article, Einstein poses the question of whether it is advisable for one who an expert on economic and social issues is not to express views about socialism. His answer to his own question is a definite yes, and he goes on further to explain why this is so, using the differences that exist in the methodological approaches used for the purpose of improving our scientific knowledge of astronomy and economics. Had he not fallen into the same trap as millions of different experts do, about the issue of what is and what is not democracy, his question would have been different, namely, whether it is advisable for one who is not an expert on economic and social issues to talk about democracy. Today he is not around to answer his own question, but I am sure that his answer would have been the same.

Why then, in his desperation, did he take socialism to be a worthy alternative to capitalism, even though he did at that time express his concerns about the dangers of a socialist government being taken over by bureaucracy? The answer to this question is to be found in his own article, where, concerned about the power and the tentacles of capitalism, he concludes that the latter **"cannot be effectively checked even by a democratically organized political society. This is true since the members of legislative bodies are selected by political parties, largely financed or otherwise influenced by private capitalists who, for all practical purposes, separate the electorate from the legislature. The consequence is that the representatives of the people do not in fact sufficiently protect the interests of the underprivileged sections of the population. Moreover, under existing conditions, private capitalists inevitably control, directly or indirectly, the main sources of information (press, radio, education). It is thus extremely difficult, and indeed in most cases quite impossible, for the individual citizen to come to objective conclusions and to make intelligent use of his political rights."** It is clear from this that he regarded a republican system of government, which is what the American system is, as being a democratic one.

In a democratic system of government private capital cannot pose any threat to the workings of democracy, since political power is in the hands of the politicians, and not in the hands of capitalists, as has already been shown. In the republican system of government, where the voting of politicians takes place, we have professional politicians who need to be elected and reelected, whereas in a democratic system of government politicians are selected by lot and for a single term only. This effectively breaks down all the tentacles of capitalism, with the proviso that the political parties move from electing to selecting with regard to all the different political officers for the various party organs, and change the way party leaders are elected as we explain elsewhere. Moreover, in a democratic system the access of political parties to the media is constitutionally ensured, and all necessary funding is provided to them by the government, as is explained in other sections of this book.

Now in view of all these, and since Einstein explains why non-experts can take part in a discussion about economic and social issues, he would have selected Democracy as the only viable alternative to capitalism! This would be so, even though discussion among participants, where voting is involved, should be restricted to those of equal strength concerning, at least, knowledge and experience. Otherwise, the whole thing is in danger of leading to undemocratic results, as we so often see happening. Furthermore, as we explain elsewhere in this book, a democratic process using also a similar educational system as the one proposed by Einstein, is the only one capable of progressively changing the capitalistic culture that is today instilled into the members of our societies.

**The question that arises, and it is pressing one, is what can one do to improve the situation in America?**

For one thing, using the same tools will not bring about change. In this highly competitive field, the opponents are far stronger, because they have more and better means to fight back. In addition, every citizen fighting for democracy should read Laurence Lessing's book, or books of this kind, so they know what is really happening, and how the game is played. It is important to know where you are, so that you do not get lost along the path to democracy. If you don't know where you are, or which way you want to go, you will never know that you are lost. All the above are, essentially, symptoms which are produced by the political instrument called voting. Unfortunately, there are many (in fact, more than half of those eligible to vote) who believe that by holding elections we automatically make sure democracy is protected. However, the facts presented above point to quite the opposite.

Some people blame the press and the various news channels for many of the evils enumerated above. It is true that these sources, which are reporting and producing news, do contribute to a very high degree to the formation of public opinion. And it is true that not all of them contribute in a positive way to the proper reporting of news. But who gives them the opportunity, in the first place, to do what they are doing? Isn't it the political parties which call for the development and expansion of such centers of information? Isn't it the need of political parties to win rather than lose votes, and the need of their candidates for office, or for the renewal of their term in office, combined with the way that election funding is done, that create the incentives for investments in this area by those who have the capability? The political parties, therefore, by accepting the political instrument of voting in order to serve democracy, effectively ruin the prospects for a democratic way of governing to prosper.

The question then arises: Is there some other means which can substitute the voting process, and offer better chances for democracy to prosper? The answer to this question is a clear and resounding yes!

Let us imagine what would happen in a situation where the candidates for office are not elected but are being selected by lot and for one term only. Their party will need money to stay in business (we will see later where the money for the party is to come from), yet the candidates themselves will no longer need to spend millions of dollars to be elected. If the party gets the required percentage of votes, a candidate will achieve political office in, say, Congress. Now a voter, who is addicted, as most voters are, to the old way of sending someone to Congress, will call this new way an anathema to the democratic process, while the framers will start turning in their graves, screaming and crying, "what, ignore the "will" of the people?" The will of the people is not being ignored. Their will is expressed when they make a choice of a party based on its national and local program. But the voter is still not happy with that. He or she prefers to select the candidate for the office, and not any party leader or any cliques within or outside the party, and he or she, also, wants primaries for that. However, the voting process is an evil process, because of the collusion it gives rise to. We have already demonstrated the results produced to this day by the voting process. Collusion goes hand in hand with the voting process, and no voter in his or her right mind will want to allow this to happen if they knew what was really happening. Nevertheless, he or she wants to make sure that the candidate for Congress, or for any other legislative body, is the right one from the perspective of being a competent one. Voters must understand that the candidate, in his or her effort to be elected, is bound to make sure that they have many more partners than just the one voter. The candidate makes sure that some of their other partners are going to make every effort to convince voters to vote for them, and, at the end of the election, they emerge not as the voters' own choice, but as the choice of the other partners. By now, the voter may be already having second thoughts about the wisdom of the old way of going about selecting legislators. Judging from the fact that not even 50% of the eligible voters go to vote, he or she no longer believes that their vote will change anything. This is a good time to assure them that the method of sortition will select even more competent officials for Congress, than the election process may ever provide.

There is only one way to ensure that we select better and demonstrably competent candidates for congressional assemblies, or for state and local legislative bodies, while conforming to the democratic principle of political equality among the voluntary candidates. The following method will do all that:

1. We set the appropriate required qualifications for every political office.
2. We invite all party members in the electoral districts who are interested to be candidates for the legislative body concerned, to apply, provided they meet the requirements for the post.
3. We create all the different ballots that cover all societal sectors, such as education, health, business etc., which apply to the specific electoral district, and put the name of each candidate in the appropriate ballot. We draw, by lot, one name from each ballot.
4. This set of candidates, who have been selected by sortition, is examined by a committee of specialists to determine that all selected candidates fulfill the requirements, and are, also, of sound mind.
5. Subsequently, we make a second draw to select the party's candidate for that electoral district, who will serve for a single term. In the next election, the specific ballot from which the candidate is drawn is removed from the group of ballots. In this way, we give the chance for everyone to be selected in the future as the party's candidate.
6. With this procedure we terminate the profession of career politicians.
7. We eliminate the whole process of fundraising by individual candidates, thus making the election process itself very economical. Candidates won't need any of these millions of dollars anymore to run their campaign, and, most importantly, they won't need any of that help which leads to a collusive relation with party bosses, or with centers of influence outside the party. Candidates are now clean, and they stay clean, because they are all representatives of the people for a single term only. They no longer need help to renew their term in office, for there can be no renewal.

If accepted by both parties, the benefits of this procedure for democracy, and, of course, for the people, will be evident immediately. One must assume, however, that it is highly unlikely that this might happen, for the politicians in power won't accept a procedure that restricts their tenure of the legislative seat to a single term. However, nobody can prevent the formation of new parties, which would apply these deliberations to their party activities, even if the only benefit will be to inform the public that there is a better way to conduct politics. In addition, these new parties can be used as laboratories through which their members can study the current political system and search for improvements. By doing simply this, these new parties can only do good.

Parties of this type bring real hope to the general public, namely that the legislative bodies will one day acquire legislators free of collusion and corruption, legislators who will really represent the people. Under the present conditions, with single-seat electoral districts and standard gerrymandering practices, it is extremely difficult to elect congressmen or any other type of legislators, at least in the beginning. It will take some time for such a procedure to be accepted widely by a public that is highly addicted to the electoral process. The idea of multi-representational electoral districts might also be an important objective for new parties to aim for, since it would pave the way for an end to the monopoly of a bipartisan political system. Whatever the case, one cannot speak of democracy when the election of legislators is the result of single-seat electoral districts. Therefore, the long-term objective is to terminate this undemocratic way of electing legislators, and substitute it by adopting multi-representational electoral districts, through which democracy will then be truly able to operate.

If we were to now assume that the two political parties, willingly or by necessity, would also be ready to adopt the new procedures, as well as the measure of multi-representational electoral districts, then one can definitely postulate that all the political parties, legislators and candidates of all kinds, may become immune to collusion and to corruption. This will require that all party funding be derived directly from the state coffers, or awarded centrally by the American government, and that the media grant time to the parties to promote their programs and their ideas on a regular basis. Immune does not mean that collusion and corruption would be eradicated; it does, however, mean that these practices will be drastically reduced, to a level where democracy can deal with them without difficulty. At that point, one will then be able to say that America is a democratic country.

The selection of the party's presidential and vice-presidential candidate will also have to change, and there will have to be an end to all the different primaries around the country, which give rise to collusion and corruption, and where winning is the result of how much money candidates have been able to spend on the campaign. **The selection of the party's candidates, for the**

**role of president and vice president, is achieved by election.** All those who want to be their party's candidates must convince voters in all the state assemblies (where voters are party members who have been selected by sortition from the set of volunteers who meet certain criteria. See criteria for parliamentary candidates). These voters constitute the new type of electoral college: they come from all walks of life, and they have no links to any pacts of collusion and corruption. In these assemblies, candidates present their positions on all the matters that concern the people and the country, and the candidate who gets most of the votes becomes the party's nominee for the presidential elections. One must keep in mind that the voting process is used only in assemblies where the voters are the result of sortition. In assemblies such as these, the role of the media is also significantly minimized. During the period of presidential elections, time is provided by the media to all candidates, so that they may present what is no longer an individual, but a party program, which is then approved by the regional assemblies and the national convention. Throughout this process, voters are the product of sortition.

One has to understand that as a result of all these activities, party life will be now revitalized, acquiring a more protagonist role, rather than simply stemming from the party's leading figures, while the party's program is now the result of collective action which takes place across the span of the party's local organizations. In general elections, people are now no longer making a choice among the different leading figures competing with each other. They are making a choice among programs, which concern issues of development, and polices intended to serve the security and welfare of the people. In general elections there is unquestionably also competition among leading figures who are the presidential or vice-presidential candidates. These candidates, however, are no longer the result of primaries, where collusion and corruption are involved on many levels. They are the result of an election process where the voters in the regional assemblies are free of any collusion. And one more thing: real representation of the people in political institutions is now a fact. These institutional structures are now staffed by representatives wholly independent of presidents, vice presidents, or other centers of influence, for the latter's involvement in them is no longer required. Their appointment is for a single term, and it expires after four years.

Conclusion: Over the course of 216 pages, Lawrence Lessing tells us the very sad story of American "democracy." His interpretation, however, of what has caused the emergence of flaws and failings is wrong. As a result, all his suggestions for the reconstitution of democracy fall in the same trap, namely that of the instrument of democracy called **voting, which is responsible for the US having an oligarchic system of government, instead of a democratic one.** One wrong tool, and democracy is gone. That is why, despite the professor's useful suggestions, his formula can only find a fertile ground where real democracy is already in operation. There, voting for politicians is restricted only to very specific cases, where voters are selected by sortition, and are free of any collusion. The exception, as explained above, is the election of presidents or vice presidents who are chosen by the people. We should all bear in mind that hostile forces to democracy develop, not because of the actions of democracy, but as a result of the actions of oligarchic governments that parade around the globe pretending to be democratic.

**Criteria for checking the requirements for presidential or party leaders and parliamentary candidates**

Throughout this section we have discussed extensively the merits of sortition for building a strong democracy, and the deadly consequences for that same democracy of the voting process for politicians. All along, we have upheld the position that true democracy is integrally linked to sortition, the process by which the political officials should be selected. It is the instrument that goes hand in hand with democracy. Despite all the strong arguments in favor of sortition, there are some counter arguments, which, based on present conditions and experiences, may be considered by some, such as Professor Lessing, as being valid. One such argument relates to the question of how in the world we are going to select parliamentarians, whose job is very demanding, by sortition. They believe that these people must be experienced in politics. They cannot be like Donald Trump for example. In other words, they want them to be professionals. There are others who do want people like Donald Trump. They prefer candidates who are off the beaten track.

The candidates for such offices need to have a certain level of knowledge that can be accredited by academic degrees, and by experience in something. They can acquire this experience through their studies and their professional career. They also must have some experience in politics. In a democracy people do participate more in issues which have political flavor, especially people who participate in party organizations. For these two requirements we have plenty of good candidates. The candidates must represent also, if possible, all sectors of human endeavor. The method of sortition is perfect for this one. The candidates must be ethical and of sound mind. On these issues neither sortition nor election can protect us 100%, and on that we can rely on tax returns, bank accounts (anything justifying sources of wealth), and medical and court evidence. There may be additional justifiable criteria that are necessary for the final decisions, such as, for example, passing an examination that will prove good knowledge of the articles of the constitution and the rules governing parliamentary debate, or others on which a given society may have to decide by some reputable method, such as holding referendums. With all these in mind, the best candidate lists for parliament can only be secured through the method of sortition.

Naturally, if all the above requirements for parliamentary candidates are necessary, then it should be obvious that they are also necessary for presidential or party leadership candidates. Democracy demands openness, and so shall it be. Now, one should note that presidential candidates and party leadership candidates are selected not by sortition, but by election. However, their election is being held in regional assemblies, where the party voters are political officers of regional party organs, and selected by sortition, thus ensuring total independence from any other party officer, with the proviso that they satisfy similar requirements as above, if not all. In these regional assemblies each candidate for the top position must prove that they are competent for the job in question.

The above procedures are free of collusion and corruption, for the circumstances in which the election is taking place are under much better control than is the case for the elections we are used to today. None of the above political officer's need spend any money to get selected or elected to the relevant position for which they are candidates. This means that one does not need to have money in order to follow such a political path. Their decision to walk this road will not be dependent on the existence of money, for there is no need of that. Nor they will have need of any media. This is the greatness of democracy and its rules, which exist for the purpose of fulfilling one mission only, that of the welfare of the people.

Another book in circulation, entitled *How Democracies Die*, and written by Steven Lesky and Daniel Ziblatt (37), both of whom are also Harvard professors, is equally worth looking into. The authors point out from the start that democracy in America is now at risk, as a result of Trump's election to the US presidency. Their conclusion comes from the experience they have garnered by studying the fall of many of the so-called democracies in the past. Their basic thesis is that **aspiring dictators** use the election process to come to power through inside channels, as well as with the help of part of the political establishment, which, in order to retain its presence on the political stage, is happy to provide these newcomers with credibility. They state that, from the time of Mussolini and Hitler, aspiring dictators no longer engage in wars to seize power. They use the possibilities that the political system itself is giving them. People engaged in politics will benefit a lot from reading this book. **However**, my own view as to the causes that lead to these developments, is that the possibilities exploited by aspiring dictators are produced by the so-called principle of democracy called voting. Because of voting, moreover, what we had, under the best circumstances, in these supposedly democratic countries, was not democracy, but some form of republic, and this includes US "democracy." These types of democracy, because they don't serve democracy's axiomatic principles result in negative perceptions in many people regarding the value of democracy itself. True democracy prevents such phenomena from happening, either because the people are happy with the results, or because democracy will not hesitate before punishing hard any who threaten it. Phenomena like the Ku Klux Klan, the John Birch Society, and other organizations of this type are not allowed to develop in true democracies. It is the capitalist democracies that allow such phenomena to blossom, and it is under the capitalist democracies that such conditions of disorder are developed: these are the conditions that allow for the cult of political personalities, such as dictators. The devil is busy in a gale of wind. And nothing can be more frightening. It is the electoral process that throws the door wide open to aspiring dictators, that gives them opportunity to seize power, and even "legitimizes" their actions.

The authors are aware of particular moments in American history, such as the period of McCarthyism (I don't want to go much further back in the past, as they do, to the time when racism flourished for years, and still does, while, presumably, the US was enjoying the fruits of its great democracy with its famous checks and balances). They are also keenly aware of the US practice of overthrowing democracies and promoting, installing, and protecting dictatorships around the world, as has certainly been the case in my country and in Cyprus, and, alas, under a Democrat US administration, as the authors say, when their colleague Henry Kissinger, as Secretary of State, used this practice to essentially invite the Turks to invade Cyprus.

One could go on and on, the list is endless. The paradox in all this is that the distinguished Harvard professors use this history to demonstrate the immense strength of American democracy, which has survived, despite all the threats that it has faced. They believe, however, that now, and for the first time, democracy in the US is in real danger. Yet, as they well know, this democracy has been in a continuous crisis, and has produced many victims. How in the world is it possible for the authors to call a country democratic, when at the same time it overthrows, as they claim, other democracies in so many places? And what about the single-seat electoral districts, where the winner takes all, combined with gerrymandering? How does this combination define or serve the axiomatic principles of democracy? A democratic country ought to produce a multiplier effect, creating new democracies in other parts of the globe, not going around setting up dictatorships. This is not a democratic America; this is an Imperial America.

So far, the behavioral principle of the US is "each man for himself," which is an attitude foreign to democracy. It is about time we stopped talking about the great American democracy, which is responsible for so many crimes against humanity. At some point, at least, some people will have to wake up and see things as they are. If this propaganda continues to be promulgated by specialists, democracy will never come. What is more, they discredit real democracy by associating it with these oligarchic systems and their crimes, for the well-camouflaged oligarchic state, which is promoted as democracy, will, eventually, lead to a dictatorship.

As far as the role of US political parties is concerned, which are called by the authors "the gate keepers of democracy," nothing has changed. The two parties continue to monopolize the political power there, through a very undemocratic electoral law, and, as has been stated earlier, they essentially block the advent of democracy in America. The problem, however, stems mainly from the fact that the political instrument used, in order supposedly to serve democracy, serves instead, and rather well, the politicians themselves, and on a continuous basis. Once this is understood, then a potential for democracy may appear. At least the authors have made a first step by accepting the fact that today "America is no longer a democratic model"; it now remains for them to admit that it never was, and for purely factual reasons. They already certify in their own writings that "the soft guardrails of American democracy have been weakening for decades." By examining what will happen in America if

Trump wins the 2020 election, they themselves "predict that the Republican Party will make efforts to shore up the party by engineering a new white majority," something that "would, of course, be profoundly antidemocratic"—and this engineering won't be devised to last just a few years. In the South, this white supremacy, which was a Democratic Party white supremacy, lasted at least until 1965. Now, with Trump in the driving seat, the Democratic Party's role in the South will be taken over by the Republican Party, and not just in the South, but across the whole nation. Isn't this what they predict? Now is therefore the time to stop beating about the bush. Things must be seen exactly as they are, and we must fight until we reach a state of real democracy in America. Only then will the checks proposed by the authors for examining the status of democracy be justified.

Single-seat electoral districts are to be found in other so-called democracies. The United Kingdom is one of them. The American model was chosen and copied from the British model, onto which they then pasted the American constitution. They just neglected to add the monarch. The FPP system of voting (First Past the Post, meaning that the candidate with the most votes, as opposed to more than half the votes, gets elected) is used in about a third of the world's countries, mostly in the English-speaking world (USA, the United Kingdom, Canada, India, Pakistan and other countries in the former British Commonwealth). In Germany one finds the same thing, namely single-seat electoral districts. Half of the candidates are selected by the party, and the other half are elected by the people. In these and other countries the instrument called voting, and not the axiomatic principles of democracy, effectively define democracy. It is a case where a tool is being equated with universal truths! The list of such democracies (or even worse) on the planet is long. One just must look at the roster of countries in the United Nations to understand why outright dictatorships are promoted as democracies. This is justified by the fact that elections are used to elect dictators, such as Maduro for example, who are in this manner given legitimized status with the people's own approval.

FPP can be used for single-member and multi-representational electoral divisions. In a single-member election, the candidate with the highest number (but not necessarily a majority) of votes is elected. In a multi-representational election (or multiple-selection ballot), each voter casts up to as many votes as there are positions to be filled, and those elected are the highest-ranked candidates that correspond to the number of available positions. For example, if there are three vacancies, then voters cast up to three votes, and the three candidates with the greatest number of votes are elected.

The voting method of multiple-round election (run-off) uses the FPP voting method in each of two rounds. The first round, held according to block voting rules, determines which candidates may progress to the second and final round (source: Wikipedia).

Because many countries use this system, it is crucial for the proposed system of government which will be developed in the next chapter that it should be adopted by those who want real change. As we have seen, the proposals of Steven Lesky and Daniel Ziblatt, while important, are being promoted using the same tools which are responsible for the mess we are facing today. In order to strengthen the applicability of any new way of implementing change, it is necessary to present here the ideas of Oxford University Professor Paul Collier (12), which are to be found in his book entitled *The Future of Capitalism* (HarperCollins, New York). His approach is to **manage capitalism**. His ideas are very sound and pragmatic, as he would say, but he too is basing his desired success on using similar tools to those that are responsible for today's mess. In a way, he also criticizes the "politicians, newspapers, magazines and so on for their sound proposals …. [which do no more than] address only one aspect of the new anxieties." Professor Collier is an economist, and he knows quite well how capitalism operates in the form in which we know it today, and he certainly pinpoints its sins very successfully. However, as he states, **"if capitalism is to work for everyone it needs to be managed to deliver purpose as well as productivity."** And yet, once it is free of its sins, which will make its production model useful for our societies, should capitalism continue to be called capitalism? Personally, I don't care what its name will be. I care only about what it may be able to provide to societies. Inevitably, his proposal to manage capitalism will meet the resistance of the *economic man*. I use the expression "every man for himself," from the first edition of my own book, *In search of a model for democracy today* (in Greek; Kaktos, Athens 2016), because it is important to bring to light the fact that the economic man is fundamentally a barbarian humanoid, which has been constructed by the capitalist model of production. Capitalism has ensured that there is a good stock of fine economists, engineers, doctors, and anything else that is profitable, but it purposefully does not produce cultured human beings who would also be oriented towards the common good of everyone belonging to a community whose members recognize that they do not have only rights, but obligations as well. As things stand today, the values of the economic man differ substantially from those of a cultured man. One just must look at the academic programs offered at universities to see why this is happening. For this reason, I cannot be hopeful that the good efforts of Professor Collier will meet with success, for he overlooks what Charles Crosland (38) also overlooked, even though he worked on the basis that **if something does not work you change it**. He overlooked the fact that what did not work was democracy, and democracy did not work because it was not a democracy to begin with. The trick of defining democracy on the basis of the so-called principle of democracy, namely voting, has discredited democracy to such an extent that it is necessary to invent a new political man, the social democrat, as though democracy did not include intrinsically the social aspects, when democracy is the only system that can create a cultured community.

The way Professor Collier constructs his proposal in order to go from the selfish genetic trait to the ethically aware community is fascinating. He uses the tenets of the Nobel Laureate Vernon Smith, "who saw that the Wealth of Nations and *The Theory of Moral Sentiments* by Adam Smith (39) are built on a common idea: the mutual benefit from exchange. The arena for exchanging commodities is the market. The arena for exchanging obligations is the networked group." By using the word arena, Vernon Smith brings to light, wittingly or not, the problem associated with the process of exchange. Underlining conditions influence the process of exchange. This is a very fine point which has always been underestimated by analysts. Adam Smith's exchange market of commodities and obligations is like a copy-and-paste duplicate of the invention of the citizens' assembly by the ancient Athenians. The Athenians thought that through the citizens' assembly they had direct democracy, and Adam Smith thought he had a free market provided there were freedom in the exchange process. Alas, neither did we have democracy, nor do we have a free market. However, the citizens' assembly was far superior as regards the promotion of democracy, than was Adam Smith's market in promoting a free exchange. This is so because the sessions of the citizens' assembly were held for about 35 days over the course of each year, and the rest of the time democracy was served by the parliament, with its well-known characteristics, namely its being free of any collusion, while Adam Smith's market was, and still is, under no effective control by the appropriate authorities, to judge from the way that the distribution of created wealth is effectuated.

One also observes arbitrary statements, such as "morality stems from our sentiments, not reason," on the assumption that sentiment and reason are managed by two totally independent centers. They are not quite independent, however. If one does not use logic, how is it possible for one to justify the existence of sentiment? Empathy for others is created just because there is logic. New scientific understanding does explain the connection between the two. The bridging of the physical part, which, obviously, includes the DNA, with the realm of the psyche, is made possible by the plasticity of the brain (*see* Francois Answered-Pierre Magistretti, *The Trace of Experience*) (40). Through this bridge, information is carried in both directions. This information constitutes the personal experience of everyone, which is saved on man's "storage disk." This experience is unique for every individual, and it makes them different from all other individuals on earth, including their family members.

What is important here is not to work away from sentiment, but towards this interconnection between reason and sentiment, which will present itself as a better and more useful alternative to a society of humanoids. This alternative perspective will be created only in a truly cultured society, and a cultured society can result only through the workings of a true democracy. Professor Collier in the third part of his book tries to approach this question, but he fails to avoid the famous trap, which is considered by many as the "principle" of democracy, namely the tool called voting!

Professor Collier does a very good job explaining "how reciprocity emerges." As we have said, an individual, in addition to any rights, also has obligations towards their fellow citizens. In most known democracies in the Western world the situation is under the control of the capitalist model of production. It was mentioned earlier that educational programs are determined at every level by the capitalist model of production. It is capitalism that imposes constraints on individuals. Having said that, the following question arises: how will the parents of a family know how to pass on to their children knowledge which they have not themselves acquired before? And even if they have this knowledge, would they have the incentive to pass on this narrative to their children, who will have to face a society whose values are defined by the capitalist system? The professor's advice is right, but that is not enough. It needs the support of a real democracy, which will ensure that there are appropriate educational programs in place, so that we may begin to change the value each citizen ascribes to themselves and to their fellow human beings. For now, the equal rights principle, which implies also the keeping of one's obligations towards others, is starting to mean exactly what it is. Yet all the above presuppose, quite simply, the existence of a cultured society, which our so-called democracies (which produce the economic man) cannot deliver. In other words, the whole thing reminds me of the legend associated with the Bridge of Arta, a town in north-west Greece: the workmen would build it during the day, and during the night some "magical" forces would tear it down.

Paul Collier's book provides a true education to those who fight for real democracy. In the current environment, this book can be a guiding tool so that, through a truly democratic process, we may get faster to an appropriate standard of culture in our society.

# Chapter Three

---

**3.1 Political Parties: Organizational Structure & Operation**

The previous chapters have prepared the ground for the next steps, which will help us reach the proposed solution of a therapy for the so-called democracies, which, as some specialist confirm, are dying. The institution of democracy serves states that care about the welfare of their people. However, as we have said, democracy can also serve all kinds of social groups. All sorts of unions exist that cover almost every aspect of human activity. In the political sector, such unions are the political parties. It has also been said that all political instruments are designed for the purpose of serving one or more of the objectives of the union, and for this reason they are prone to changes when the objectives of the union are not served.

One of the axiomatic principles of democracy relates to the political equality of the members of a union. This criterion of equality must be upheld in every process that has to do with the staffing of all the political institutions which a democratic system uses for its proper function. It is evident that if the system deliberately creates a political institution, it is so that it can operate properly. For this latter to occur, the candidates who will staff a political institution, such as a party organ, or parliament, or the position of party leader etc., must meet certain meritocratic, and non–meritocratic, criteria. (a) They must be volunteers, in the sense that they are not drafted against their will. (b) They meet all the requirements for the job. This is done in order to ensure the proper functioning of the institutions of democracy, so that they can serve in turn, in the best way possible, their main objective, which is the welfare of all the people of the union. This means that the overall composition of the manpower of these institutions must satisfy the condition that all voices are being heard within a given environment. As a result, the range of its members must be such that their knowledge and experience are of similar quality, in addition to satisfying the social and geographical criteria. This prerequisite is a must, in order to avoid giving rise to circumstances like those in the citizen's assemblies of ancient Athens, where some voices were never heard, because the deliberations were usually under the control of the more educated and experienced orators. (c) The staff of these institutions must be selected by sortition, except for the position of party leaders, where the selection is done by voting in all the regional party assemblies, and whose voters are the result of sortition.

"The density of political organizations which, after all, are agents of political mobilization, also seem to be related to youth turnout, although in this case the results are contradictory. Countries with high levels of party membership show lower levels of electoral participation among young people than countries with low levels of party membership. Conversely, the presence of high union density is associated with a high level of turnout (91.3% compared to 76.1%).

Finally, another factor that seems to increase the level of electoral participation among the young is their level of politicization. Those that are interested in politics, or feel close to a party, or are members of political organizations show a higher turnout than young citizens without these attributes (87.2% compared to 74.1%)."

## Is Electoral Abstention a Problem of Democracy?

In their report researchers state also that "elections play a vital role in a system of representative democracy. They are the primary mechanism with which to implement the principle of popular sovereignty. Ultimate authority rests with the people and the people delegate this authority to government representatives through the electoral process." This statement, however, sounds more like a joke. Everybody knows that ultimately authority rests, in practice, with the few, while on paper it only rests with the people; this is the real problem of democracy. Either the researchers at International IDEA are totally naïve, or they are trying to hide something which cannot be hidden. And the report continues: "Periodic elections provide citizens a means to replace incumbents and change the government. Thus, they help the public to keep officeholders and political parties accountable." The researchers haven't probably heard of gerrymandering.

Yet in the existing democracies, we know that we are not politically equal, even when the principle of political equality is explicitly written in the constitution of every contemporary democracy. The declarations and bylaws of all political parties also affirm that all their members are politically equal, but we know that they are not; one could go on at great length. The counterargument presented by many is that this principle applies to democracies where free elections are held. Every citizen can vote, and each vote carries equal weight. This, however, is the one thing that does not happen and, unfortunately, under the present political conditions, such voting does not serve democracy, because what most voters vote for does not represent an opinion formed in some party assembly, but the view of those who serve the well-known centers of influence. That is why, in practice, the above claim has no real value. It is well known how the media can sway many voters as regards what and for whom to vote, especially the media that are being controlled by powerful economic centers. In addition, many voters make personal deals with the candidates. These deals involve the exchange of some form of favor, which implies the existence of collusion of some kind. The first thing we need to examine, therefore, is whether political equality among party members exists, not just on paper, but also in real life.

**The ancient Athenians resolved the issue of political equality, which should be a serious concern for all political parties, using sortition for the selection of all holders of political office, and they restricted these appointments to a single term.** This tool proved itself to be of value in practice, and there is good and significant reason to assume that, in good time, political parties may come to adopt it. An article by Professor Alessandro Pluchino, of the Department of Physics and Astronomy at the University of Catania, in Italy, written in collaboration with others, argues that even if only half of the members of the Italian parliament were selected randomly for only one term, the parliament would work more democratically and more efficiently than it does currently.

In ancient Athens they did not have political parties of the type we have now. We should, therefore, examine that period in greater detail, and see if we can use political parties today in the way tribes were used in Athens.

To start with, we can begin by looking at the reforms undertaken by **Cleisthenes** in 508 B.C. He formed ten new tribes, which were to serve as electoral districts. The method he used to form them has been explained in a previous chapter. All districts covered the entire territory of the city–state, and they also had the same population, which consisted of a particular admixture of citizens coming from the entire city–state, as has already been explained earlier. **Cleisthenes'** reforms combined the population of Attica in such a way as to break at least some of the ties people had within their original four tribes, some of which were family tribes while others consisted of people hailing from specific geographical areas.

Some writers consider these reforms as revolutionary, perhaps because they were carried out under the same conditions that had also brought **Cleisthenes** to power. Eventually, these reforms consolidated the new territories and the overall structure of the city-state of Athens (Attica), but they also brought to the surface the true tensions underlying the relations between the various groups, namely the struggle between the democrats (most of them poor) and the rich. In any case, as we have already seen in the first chapter, these reforms did not install democracy, nor did they break the ties of kinship or common origin; all they did was to define more clearly the boundaries of the city-state. **Democracy came truly into force when the implementation of sortition was extended to include the selection of all holders of public office.**

In order to understand this point better, let us look more closely at the new configuration of the tribes brought about by Cleisthenes' reforms. The composition of their population was such, that even citizens who might be living in the same building could belong to different tribes. These tribes were actually put together in a purely structural way, and only for the purpose of assigning to them political characteristics similar to those assigned to the electoral districts of today, with one difference, however, namely they all covered the same territory, that of the city-state. The original four tribes continued to exist, and in fact they oversaw most of the traditional cultural or religious practices. In no way, therefore, could this new kind of reconfiguration of the ten tribes have cut all the umbilical cords of dependency among the citizens in the original four tribes; horizontal interdependence (two-way dependency) of citizens would have continued to be in full force, if the institutional mechanism of sortition, which abolishes almost all incentive for interdependence, had not been introduced. Each tribe's new demographic composition contained also individuals living far from one another, and it included also poor, middle class, and wealthy people, who were competing among themselves for the improvement of their individual economic and social position; they were, of course, all Greeks, either by birth or through naturalization.

If we now examine the composition of any political party, we will realize that it is somehow more homogeneous as far as its members are concerned, because they belong to the same ideology, even though they may not be so homogeneous as regards their social status, whereas the composition of ancient political tribes was not homogenous at all. So by using the method of sortition to select, let's say, the 50 members of parliament who would represent the tribe, the probability of selecting a set of parliamentarians that did not represent the entire spectrum of trends (political, geographical or social), or one that represented some more strongly than others, is quite high, or is at least possible. On the other hand, if we examine now the case of the political parties, we observe that we have in each a specific ideology, whereas the members are scattered all over the nation, and the same holds as regards their social status. Based on these observations one can easily surmise that sortition, when applied to political parties for the purpose of selecting holders of political office, will give far better results with respect to the group synthesis of the members selected in this way. In this manner one will achieve within the party a much better representation of the people who support it.

If we examine the results of parliamentary elections, the synthesis of the members of parliament will be much more representative of the people, than the one that was obtained in the case of the tribes in ancient Greece. Of course, one must adapt in the case of political parties the phrase "they were all Greeks" so that it reads "they are all Greek conservatives," or Greek socialists or whatever might be applicable. This is true, even though party ideology takes a back seat in almost every case today, regardless of all the party leadership's declarations when promoting their policies, and this is true especially with some parties, when they come to power. A corollary result that ensues from this, namely the diminishing role of ideology in political parties today, is that as the number of political parties in a country increases, the chances of cooperation among them become correspondingly higher, especially during parliament voting. This is what has happened recently also in Germany, where the Christian Democrats and the Social Democrats are cooperating even on a governmental level. One can see the same practice in Greece, Spain, and Italy, as well as in several other countries. On the other hand, in countries where we have only two parties, cooperation seems to be extremely difficult. Each party seeks to secure the majority in order to be in power, and the dividing line between the two parties becomes significantly more demarcated. In the US this phenomenon is taking on a particularly ugly form.

It is important to examine again at this point the political instrument of the citizens' assembly, and to see how such a tool might work in the case of political parties. An assembly of this type could take place in the local constituency of a political party, where the number of party members does not rise above one hundred, or at a regional or even national level; an example would be the party's regional or national congress. One thing to note is that regardless of the level, the debate between those who take the floor to speak will only be among conservatives in a conservative party, or only among socialists in a social democratic party, or only among democrats, or republicans etc., because of the state of homogeneity that exists in the assembly as far as ideology is concerned. By contrast, in the citizens' assembly in the direct democracy of ancient Athens the debate was mainly between aristocrats and the wealthy during the first century of democracy, whereas during the century that followed one could also see a combination of several things. On this basis, anyone with any amount of experience can easily conclude that, as far as the operational aspect is concerned, the party members' assembly is superior to the citizens' assembly of ancient times. Also, because voters in the regional and national party assemblies are the result of sortition, the decisions made in those assemblies through voting will reflect to a considerable extent the wishes of the members of the party.

Regarding the question whether the party's members are free of collusion or not, in the case of a party members' assembly at a local constituency, because the number of the participants is small, collusion is rather limited, also because the party members of a local organization know one other. However, if sortition is not used as expected, the situation may change radically for all the members' assemblies of a party, whether they take place at a local, regional or national level. All this happens of course because of the competition among party members, in order to increase their influence over the party membership for the purpose of securing, through elections, positions of power within the party. This sort of competition, which is associated with elections, constitutes the mechanism by which collusion is produced, not only among the members of a party, but also between party members and external centers of influence. Such practices were taking place among the aristocrats during the deliberations of the citizens' assembly in the direct democracy of Athens, and at an even more intense level, when votes were being held for the election of specialists, or for the passing laws, or decrees, or other things. That is why democracy was not free to operate then, and why it is not free to operate today. For one thing, the axiomatic principle of democracy that stipulated political equality among equals was totally disregarded because of the voting process, something that has serious repercussions on the workings of democracy. More importantly, some voices were never herd.

At this point, we need to look more closely at the composition of political parties in order to understand the use of this marvelous tool of sortition. In this analysis we will use the Greek parties as an example, even though it makes no difference which country's parties we examine. From the very start of their formation, one observes in most political parties' certain practices, especially on the part of the members of the top executive committee, which are aimed at increasing their personal influence over the party membership at a national level. In this way, they ensure that when elections for the different national or local party structures take place, these members will help them increase their power within those structures, something which will be beneficial to them in the future. All these practices are organized under the cover of so-called democratic elections. As a result, we observe right from the beginning the formation of cliques within the party (whether ideological or not, some may even be for the specific purpose of corruption), which give rise to internal party "wars." The intention is to pave the way so that particular individuals can succeed to the top position in the party, when the time comes for the party leader to step down. This is exactly how "democracy" works in political parties. These rivalries, unfortunately, also involve the media, and a variety of outside centers of influence. Party members maintain that the result, since it derives from elections, is by definition democratic. Alas, these are the worst possible results that could ever have been produced by "free" elections. The party structures, staffed with members appointed in this manner, are usually built using the worst possible "components," not only from the point of view of competence, but also from the point of view of ethics. Deliberations of this kind create, especially within the party, a very negative climate for decent and competent people who want to serve the lofty aims of the party from a position of political office. Under such conditions, they avoid getting involved, and, therefore, keep away from participating in such processes, for there is a risk that they might become involved in elections in which cliques are heavily implicated, and thus influence unwittingly the outcome of the election results. This would compromise them in the eyes of their fellow members, and, even worse, more generally in the eyes of those with whom they live and work.

These conditions in the long run result in the complete discreditation of the political parties. A party's good name, with time, loses its attractiveness for the electorate; and once they start losing elections, the time comes to change even the party's name: as they say, once it can no longer have the same number of followers as before, its life cycle has come to an end. The most disturbing effect of such developments is the people's disappointment, as former supporters in these cases may not just abandon their party, but also politics altogether. This situation is happening worldwide, and as a result many people are not even using their vote. In some countries, abstention reaches levels as high as half of those eligible to vote, or even more. **Be wary of parties changing names, for they intend to bury old sins by hiding behind a new face.**

**What should then be done to overcome such scheming practices that take place within all political parties through, as they claim, democratic procedures and free elections (which, as we have seen, lead to such catastrophic results)?**

A party that operates democratically and is transparent about the truth towards its followers and the electoral body, has no need to change its name. After all, a good party, through years of activity, builds a strong reputation, which should not be discounted. Unfortunately, all political parties around the world today suffer from the same disease. Their internal operations and actions are not conducted democratically, and their reputation gradually declines, before it eventually vanishes, for the reasons explained above. This undemocratic conduct is not limited only within the party, but it is constantly being transmitted beyond it to society, whereby the familiar undesirable results are produced. It is for these reasons that many organizations working for the protection of the environment, or for better living conditions, or for human rights, etc., are against political parties in general, and promote instead some form of citizens' assembly, thinking that this will work better. We have expanded on this earlier above.

A political party is a very good tool for the operation of democracy with the proviso that parties will be reformed. This reform concerns the type of process used to select the holders of political office in all political parties. One should not forget that the holders of political office in all party structures make very important political decisions that affect our lives, and we want them to be free of any dependency or collusion. The issue therefore is not simply an organizational matter that only concerns the party. The issue is a highly political one. This required step of reform, which is a giant step in the direction of democratic rule, will lead to what it is needed for democracy to work for the benefit of all in every society. Party leaders, instead of simply making declarations in favor of democracy, should do something that will set democracy back on the right track.

Before we tackle the important issue of reform in political parties, we have to take a step back and remind ourselves of the reason why party leaders or aspiring party leaders use the above practices while performing their "duties": **It is all about human nature**! This is what we need to overcome. At present, our societies are addicted to a certain way of life and conduct, which have been inculcated in the citizens of every society by the very actions of today's democracies. The main characteristic of this way of life and conduct is the attitude of every man for himself. It leads to wars, crimes, and to a high level of social unrest. The unjust distribution of the wealth produced is one of the primary causes of the social conditions we are facing today. This means that our democracies are not working properly. And if democracies are not working properly, it also means that the people's cultural level in a society declines because of neglect on the part of democracy. This is when the democratic system breaks down, and our societies turn into sheer jungles. This is where we are now. The remedy for setting democracies back on the right track consists of reforms which must start at the level of political parties. There is no other way, except to take collusion and, to a certain degree, corruption, out of the present system, and there is a way to accomplish this.

All forms of collusion and corruption, as has been already mentioned, are initially produced within the political parties. The politicians, in their effort to survive and renew their term in power, do not hesitate to totally forget and disregard the axiomatic principles of democracy. The usual facade they employ to cover their undemocratic, and sometimes criminal, activities is to use elections, which they can successfully manipulate with the assistance of well-established cliques inside the parties, and, when needed, with the assistance of outside centers of influence (which, by the way, also benefit from having "their" people in positions of power). In this way, they kill two birds with one stone. The stone is the "democratic" election; the birds are the renewed terms for those holding public office, so they can continue their "democratic" work, and collect the benefits that such positions of power can yield for them. This process goes endlessly on and is very costly. What is more infuriating, is that the cost, and much more that accrues from having to repay the favors to their supporters, is paid by the people.

This situation can change. We do not need to become involved in revolutions, but we do need, however, to engage in a peaceful process. This engagement begins and ends simply with supporting political parties that operate within a framework that truly produces and satisfies all the axiomatic principles of democracy.

The existing parties will not be easily convinced to change their habits. But voters can make them or break them by switching their support to parties that meet the requirements of a party that operates democratically. This involves some of the steps the ancient Athenians had taken. **They used sortition instead of election for the purpose of selecting all holders of political office and for one term only.** In our times, all we must achieve, as a first step, is the selection of every party officer, for every party structure, at any level, using sortition, and for one term only. This reform will automatically start weeding out of the political process all collusion and most of the corruption produced today. The reason is simple. There is no incentive anymore for any party officer to get involved in acts of collusion or corruption for the purpose of getting help to renew his or her term, or in order to be promoted to higher positions. Nobody can help them. At the end of their term they return to what they were doing before. It is as simple as that. The ancient Athenians, from the time of Ephialtes, selected members of parliament, leaders of tribes, and sworn jurists using lots. Their objective was to get collusion and corruption out of the system of government.

A party that abides by the principles of democracy and wants to serve them well, needs to do no more than to adopt these reforms and operate according to these rules in order to select all of its political officers, who will then staff its various structures, except the party leader. Those members of the party who are interested in serving in any of the party structures, and who meet at the same time the requirements stated clearly in the bylaws of the party, will need to declare their willingness to the party. These members should preferably come from every walk of life and reflect the level and quality of the living standards of society. If color or race are present in this society, then representative candidates from these groups will also appear on the long list. If the party leader then wishes to convene a party body, such as a national congress, or a central committee, etc., all they need to do is use the method of sortition (drawing of lots) to select all the members of any structure, women and men in equal numbers, if they so wish.

This change does not require any amendments in the existing laws of the nation. If a political party wants to make these reforms for the purpose of democratizing itself, all that is mainly needed is the will of the leadership. This kind of outreach on the party's side towards the members of society will especially increase the interest of those who have abandoned politics altogether, because they felt that nothing could be done to change things. They will realize that they do not have to compete with the existing party cliques anymore in their effort to be selected to any of the party structures, as is being done now. A party that will take such steps to reform itself can increase people's interest even more if, in addition to adopting the method of sortition for selecting members for any of its structures, it also aims at improving their synthesis and quality. On the basis of living standards, which reflect the level of infrastructure in the fields of education, health, etc. in a particular region, the party can choose by lot one member for each sector of human activity in that region, if the intention is to form a local constituency, or more than one member, if the intention is to form a regional or a national congress of the party. This is the method that was used in ancient Athenian democracy – and it worked. The term of these political structures may be one, two, or four years at the beginning. Later on, once the party has acquired more members, it can decrease the time in office in order to give a chance to all eligible members of the party to become officers, if they so wish, provided they meet the required criteria for the post.

A local constituency of any party will consist of ordinary party members and the administrative council, whose members are now selected by sortition from the group of the local constituency's volunteers who wish to serve in it. We now have a kind of citizens' assembly which is far better than the type that was used by the ancient Athenians. For one thing, it is much smaller, and it can thus be very effective, while the group synthesis of its members will be much more homogeneous. During its deliberations, because it is now vested with powers as prescribed by the by-laws of the party's organization, it can vote on and make decisions about the local development program, or about the positions of the party on other issues concerning the local region. Such citizens' assemblies will operate in all the local constituencies across the nation. If this were now to happen in every party, we would have thousands of such citizens' assemblies working for the national program of each party. These kinds of reforms will also greatly regenerate interest in members of society who have abandoned politics, and we will witness an increase of people returning to politics, for they will see at last that their voices are being heard and taken seriously into consideration for the first time. As regards the national congress of any party, whose members are selected from each region also by sortition, the only decisions it will have to take will mainly concern the prioritization of each section of the program, and the time-tabling of its implementation. Horizontal grassroots movements, such as those which are concerned about the environment, or the ending of wars, or what have you, either form distinct political parties, or join existing but reformed parties, where they can now be more effective. The same holds true for all different types of syndication. In this way, all decisions will be taken within the national parliament, and not outside it, as is being done today, a method which, unfortunately, causes many injustices, such as the unequal treatment of certain social groups, or the unequal distribution of wealth etc. In the new national parliament, where all voices will be represented, all voices will be heard, and that alone makes it superior to any citizens' assembly where many voices may not ever be heard.

Members coming from all over the nation, if they aspire to become party leaders, will have to be highly competent and demonstrate their leadership qualities to the majority of the party membership when they run for office through an election. This process will no longer be the result of the machinations of scheming cliques, as they exist and operate today within the parties. There will be no incentive anymore for any member of the party to promote cliques, for there won't be any benefit: members of the party structures are selected by sortition and not by election, where cliques usually dominate. Cliques can no longer promote their members to positions of power in party structures, nor renew their term in office. At the same time, with this method, all members of the party acquire broad experience, which is useful both for the party and for society, since such participation in party assemblies will begin to raise the cultural standard of the party members, which is one of the primary objectives of a true democracy. It is the improvement of the cultural level of the people that will also resolve the issue of the unjust distribution of created wealth. We will come back to this issue further below.

In this model, those who vote for the party leader, namely ordinary members and the members of party structures who have been selected by sortition, are totally independent of any party bosses. In fact, there are no party bosses any longer, nor any external influences on the party members: there is no longer demand for such services from anyone who holds any position within the party structure, or from an external center of influence, given that there are no more elections, since all positions in party structures are filled by sortition and for one term. The incumbents earn their position in any party structure through sheer luck. External centers of influence can only use money in order to buy votes, something nobody can stop (and I am not going to dispute that such danger exists), but now the buyers have to spend an enormous amount of money, because they have to pay more and perhaps even higher inducements, instead of buying off just the leadership of the party, as is being done today. The image of the candidates for party leadership can be tarnished or embellished by external centers of influence the way things work today, and such skewed portrayals may influence some members of the party, which of course is not a desirable outcome. For these reasons, changes in this area are necessary, and some ideas about how to effect those changes will be proposed later in this chapter. However, if the political parties were to proceed with the reforms that lie within their own sphere of influence, then the situation as regards the media would also change in a positive way. First, politicians won't need them at all, the way they do today, except to promote the party. Some politicians may complain about the conduct of the media, but we should not forget that it is the politicians' own needs that are responsible for the expansion of this huge market. It is the voting process for the election of politicians, or for their re-election and renewal of their term in office, that opens this can of worms.

Coming back to the reforms that are needed, some of their detractors may claim that with this method the party structures are not being staffed by competent members. The answer to this argument has already been given elsewhere, where it has been shown that the probability for this to happen is very low. On the other hand, however, who would claim that cliques, which are formed secretly and operate secretly, are made up of only competent members? **From a wealth of personal experience, I can attest that they are not. Worst of all, however, many party officers owe their victory to party bosses or to centers of influence outside the party. Maybe the only argument that will convince those who reject the use of sortition is to invoke the wonders achieved by the ancient democracy of Athens, despite the problems created by the citizens' assembly. These wonders are the very foundation of Western civilization.** There is a "paradox" here, in that the same axiomatic principles which were followed by the parliament in the democracy of Athens so as to implement the decisions taken in the citizens' assembly, are not being upheld by parties in power today, despite the fact that the very same principles have been enshrined in the constitutions of all the so-called democracies around the world.

One more issue that needs to be addressed concerns the election of the party leader by vote, instead of by lot. This different tune causes some dissonance in the melody as a whole; however, I am proposing sound arguments for this exception. Firstly, the leaders of the ancient tribes were also elected. This rule, however, was later changed – according to some sources, by Ephialtes' reforms. I found no conclusive information as to whether this reform improved the administration of Athens, or whether things continued as they did before the change. The second reason why I want to keep a process of election for the leader of the party is that they will be henceforth elected by assemblies on a regional basis, where (a) all voting members are now totally independent from one another and from outside centers of influence, through the use of sortition and the limitations of the single term in office, and (b) all candidates for the position of party leader must develop their ideas, and put forward proposals to the assembly members on each and every topic, concerning all the sectors that together determine the overall standard of living in the region in question. The quality of the proposals made in these assemblies by the candidate for every sector of human activity can open the way to the leadership of the party. This procedure is repeated across the country's regions. The two forerunners, if no one has claimed more than 50% of the votes, then run against each other in a one-day election that takes place within one or two weeks, and all-party members can take part and vote in this runoff. Let us be reminded that all the voters now have a much more empowered role than the one voters had in the citizens' assembly in the city-state of Athens, when they were voting for the ten generals or for other important specialist positions, since they are totally independent from party bosses or other external centers of influence. Ultimately, through the use of sortition, party leaders are stripped of many of the authorities they now have over their members; in addition, as I will propose later on, through a change in the process of selecting the members of parliament, the new leader will need to be highly competent and very experienced to govern the party, as he or she will have to work hard to persuade the party members, instead of ruling by issuing commands. In this way, and for the first time, true democracy will prevail in the way a party is run.

Imagine if party nominees for the presidency of the USA, instead of running in primaries, where money and underhanded dealings play a central role, went to speak instead in every state in regional congresses, where voters would be the result of sortition: how different the results would have been for America today, and, what is more, how inexpensive. All of this will work towards the benefit of all.

Of course, it is not easy for an individual to act and live as a democratic member of society. We should remember Freud's dictum concerning cultured people. We can equally easily imagine how difficult it is for an entire group of people to live and act democratically. In the latter case, one must invent mechanisms of trust in order to achieve the best outcomes for the party. This brings another item to the foreground, which concerns the kind of citizen a true democracy produces. A true democrat is also a very cultured person. Ultimately, these are the kind of citizens we should be after. Andreas Schiehl and Tom Wohlfarth (41) from the German think tank *Demokratie*, examine in their work ***The Culture of Democracy*** certain factors which get in the way during the deliberations of citizens' assemblies, and outline, with the help of numerous vital questions, steps, which may be taken in a citizens' assembly in order to reach the desired results.

This sort of guidance on how best to define and delimit the deliberations of citizens' assemblies is critical for our times, since culture in most countries, if not in all, has been delegated to the back seat and to a state of hibernation. Today's version of homo sapiens can be encapsulated in the motto 'every man for himself.' No one claims that democracy is an easy system of government. However, it is much more serviceable than the alternatives, and sooner or later it will be the only system that will remain as the sole option for our survival as a species. Let us remember that good things do not come easy. For one thing, the existing political parties will offer hard opposition to such reforms and transformations. All of them are staffed by professional politicians, and accepting such party transformations is equivalent to signing their own "death warrants," for this new type of political party will lead to the abolishment of that profession for good. We have no need of professional politicians; what we need are good professionals in centers of production of wealth. As this new type of political party grows in strength, the old type will be shrinking, and either it will adapt itself to the new organizational model, or it will be forced to file for chapter 11. In the new era, the only parties that will exist will be those whose organizational models are based on the instrument of sortition for selecting, instead of electing, all single-term political officials for any party structure, even though each party may differ in ideology. These ideologies will be standing up against one another in the new type of national parliaments, whose members will also be for a single term. Now, however, they will also be free of any form of collusion. And all of this will be achieved not based on money, but thanks to the simple participation of the people!

### 3.2 Method for Selecting Members of Parliament

This proposal of how candidates for seats in parliament should be selected has the objective of ensuring that the national parliament will truly represent the people. Today this is not happening. Up to this point, all the reforms we have discussed and proposed, concerning the political parties, will require no changes to the constitution of Greece. This may hold true for many other countries as well. For Greece, the proposal for the selection of candidates for parliamentary seats presupposes some constitutional changes, if it is to have any practical value. This required change in the constitution is due to an existing article which defines the elected member of parliament as a representative of the people in the nation as a whole, and not as a representative of the party voters in the district where she or he is elected, either through the use of a preferential cross by the voter, or through the ranking position in which the candidate has been placed by the leadership on the party list. As a result of this provision in the constitution, many members of parliament elected under the umbrella of one party, switch parties as we come closer to the elections, in order to secure their own reelection. Such undemocratic misconduct on the part of parliamentarians constitutes a very bad example for the members of society who had voted for them in the previous elections, and who now see them turning into defectors, while also waving the banner of rebellion. Therefore, changing the constitutional provision so that a parliamentarian may be now defined as the representative of the electoral district and the voters that have elected him, would also place the party itself in greater alignment with the democratic principles. Objections by some to this change to the constitution, which concern the rules under which the political parties operate, are not justified. They claim that the change will increase further the power of the party leadership, which may behave as a tyrant, and totally deprive party parliamentarians of their own voice. This argument is valid based on current conditions today. However, with the party reforms, which are proposed here, the party leadership will have no such powers anymore. Democracy will finally work from within the party, and decisions will be taken mainly following the rule of majority. All parliamentarian party members will have to respect these rules, or else resign, or be forced by the majority to resign, so that the next in line on the list may become the new member of parliament for the party. The parliamentary seat does not belong anymore to a party member. It belongs to the party, because the voters now vote for the party, and not for an individual candidate. The idea is to get away from the present situation where the candidate and the voter may be connected by some form of collusion. The abhorrent phenomenon of the defector will also be finally eradicated in this way.

Having established the grounds for the required constitutional change, we can now propose the new rules under which the candidates for parliament should be selected. The method is simple: it will be conducted by sortition. The party candidate list is formed by lot from a pool of member volunteers drawn from the Development Councils of the party. The members of each Development Council are elected each year by the party members in each local constituency. Their duty is to define the local development program of the party for that region. These members come from all the local sectors of human endeavor. In a way, they are regarded as the local experts in their field, which means they must meet the requirements set by law in order to become members of parliament. The procedure followed in order to compose the list is very similar to the selection process proposed for choosing officials for the different party structures. This time, however, because we are dealing with elections (a fact that is not easy to change), we have to use the process of sortition twice: The first time round, the party leadership puts all individuals who have expressed an interest in being a region's parliamentary candidates through a screening process. This is carried out in order to ensure that all candidates meet the requirements set by law for the role. The leadership here involves the party president and the national council, whose members, as we said earlier, are selected by sortition. At this point, a process of sortition begins in order to generate the list of candidates for parliament. During the parliamentary elections, voters only choose the party; any candidate preferences indicated on the ballot by the voters are null and void. The procedure starts with the first phase which has as its objective the formation of a set of volunteers that represents as much as possible all the different sectors of production. They must be professional people, and they must also be residents of the electoral district under consideration. Once this set is formed, then the process of sortition begins, and from each sector of production one member is drawn. If, in the resulting set, the number of candidates is greater than the number of parliamentary seats set by law for the electoral district, then a further draw from among this new set takes place, until the number in the set equals that of the available parliamentary seats in the district. We have thus now managed to form the party list; whose members owe their presence on it merely to sheer luck. They do not owe their inclusion to any preferential treatment on the part of the leader or anyone else. At this point, no one knows who will be elected to parliament. In this way, all candidates on the list have a strong incentive to work hard for the party to increase the percentage of votes the party will get. The higher the percentage of votes the party receives, the more seats there will be for the party. However, if the ranking of candidates is done before the election, then those candidates who are at the bottom of the list won't have a strong incentive to work hard for the party. That is why this phase must take place after the election. After the election, the order of the candidates on the list is again determined using the method of sortition, and, depending on the party's strength following the elections, the number of parliamentarians for the party in each constituency is determined. This second round of sortition is very important, as it deprives the party leadership of any power to determine the position of the candidates on the list, and thereby exerting direct control over the parliamentarians.

This process for the selection of candidates for parliament may in some countries require a change in the electoral law. The process is very simple, and candidates do not need millions of dollars to run their campaign. As a matter of fact, they need no money at all. Each party will have free access to the local media, and every party will therefore be able to broadcast their positions and their development program to the voters. All candidates must live in the area (be permanent residents) and they must be employed in that region. Those who will be elected will serve just one term. There is no way that they could renew their candidacy for the following parliamentary elections. One can see that this kind of procedure takes collusion or corruption for the purpose of renewing one's term in office out of the picture.

The tenure of the party leaders should be handled in the way it was done by the ancient Athenians in the case of the ten generals. My proposal is that party leaders can serve for up to two terms. One term means four years. All party leaders can select their own team of specialists to help them meet the needs of the leadership. The advisors' terms of office terminate at the same time as the tenure of the party leader, and some of them may have to be excluded from being selected for any office for at least five years. The tenure of the parliamentarians follows the rules laid out in the constitution, which means that they cannot be replaced for a minimum period of four years or until the next elections.

### 3.3 The Electoral Laws

The electoral laws are a consequence of the use of the political instrument called voting, a tool that, in our days, and incorrectly, is regarded by most as being synonymous with democracy. In earlier chapters, and here, we have demonstrated that voting used to elect politicians works against the principles of democracy. Therefore, electoral laws represent monuments to despotism and autarchic behavior, especially in the case of party leaders. The fundamental logic behind it is like that of gerrymandering, namely, it is a logic that has one objective only, how to transform a minority into a majority.

In Greece, since the fall of the military junta, the electoral system has had a misleading title intended to hide what was really going on. Due to this law, Greece has always had a minority government which, by way of a 'convenient' electoral law is transformed into a majority one (the political party that has most votes is awarded additional seats in parliament). Its name ever since has been the **reinforced proportionality law.** The magical booster, known as a "majority bonus," has always been provided to ensure that the party in government will have more than 50% of the seats, even though it had considerably fewer than 50% of the votes. This system was an invention of the conservative party, now called New Democracy, right after the fall of the military junta. Depending on certain circumstances, this invention could provide the leading party with a majority of seats in parliament after it has won as little as around 36% of the votes. Thus, Greece created a fantastical democracy, where a minority rules over the majority! According to the statements of the leading party at the time, these provisions were used for the purpose of having strong governments. Later, the socialist party, the Panhellenic Socialist Movement (PASOK), made this even more glaringly obvious. Through some changes in the electoral law, it passed a clause that gave the leading party a bonus of 40 seats, which were taken away from the runner-up party. When New Democracy next came to power, it increased this bonus of seats given to the leading party from 40 to 50 (17% of the total parliamentary seats). The man who spearheaded this, a university professor and an expert in constitutional affairs, was, at the time this book was being written, the president of the Hellenic Republic.

At least, they removed the word democracy and called Greece with its proper name, namely that of a **republic**. Until a few months ago **(2016–2019)**, Greece had a "very strong" government, as a result of the bonus of 50 seats given to the leading party, which had secured roughly just one third of the elected members of parliament. More precisely, 104 deputies held 153 seats, while the remaining seats, which mathematically should be 196, were reduced to 147. **What is more offensive is that this government, a coalition of two parties, came to power with only 19% of the electorate in Greece voting for the first group (a left-wing party) and something like 3% for their partner (a party of the extreme-right).**

**No wonder that "democracies" are dying: their problem is that they were never democracies in the first place.** This does not happen only in Greece. Recently, the Brexit resolution in the United Kingdom was passed through a referendum where only 26% of the eligible voters in that country participated, and nobody batted an eyelid. For the political parties in power it is all (political) business as usual, as if nothing tragic had happened, and this is all in the name of democracy.

In 2015, I made a proposal to the Greek political parties, suggesting a change to the electoral law. Up to this day, not a single political party has come out in its favor. The philosophy behind the proposal was to bypass the argument by politicians of the leading party that Greece has no tradition in forming coalition governments. According to them, the bonus given to the first party is therefore necessary in order to have a government at all. The smaller parties, on the other hand, would rather there were no bonus, so they can blackmail their larger partners during negotiations for the formation of a coalition government, and receive more benefits for themselves, such as more ministerial posts in the cabinet. Up until very recently, the junior partner in the coalition government in Greece was able to obtain ministerial portfolios for 7 out of their 9 members of parliament!

My proposed change to the electoral law was to transform the bonus given to the leading party, which would now be far less than fifty seats, into a strong incentive for large and small parties to try and form a coalition government, by rewarding the leading party, or alliance of parties, only if they could already secure the majority of seats in parliament without the bonus. In this way, and with the provision that elections will only be held once every four years, strong governments can be formed, and with a substantial majority in parliament, without any legerdemain. The bonus seats would come from those parties refusing to form, or participate in, a coalition government.

In order to run for parliament, parties in Greece must have candidate lists in most of the nation's constituencies, and in order to elect members of parliament they must win at least 3% of the total votes cast. Similar requirements are found in the electoral laws of many countries. Some information was given in the third chapter regarding most English-speaking countries. This it is done either to avoid a proliferation of small parties, which is seen as a wise measure, or to ensure that some disturbing minority will not enter parliament. In Turkey, for example, in order to make it difficult for the Kurds to elect members of parliament, the electoral threshold is as high as 10% of the votes cast. This also means that, instead of having diverse interests represented in parliament, the establishment prefers to handle any issues involved outside parliament, and often in secrecy, through reciprocal deals between the party in power and its clients. In this way, social injustice and inequality are further fostered and, if required, approved by parliament. This is exactly where the so-called functional democracies lead: to injustice, crimes and inequalities, as we can judge from their results. I consider the use of a low electoral threshold in the electoral law as a positive measure; however, this barrier should be kept at a very low level.

In the previous chapter and in the present one, we have touched upon human nature. Partly, this results in an automatic promotion of personal interests, which receive a higher priority compared to those of the collective. For this reason, it was emphasized elsewhere that in collective decisions and actions taken by any group or society, members of that society must all benefit from the results produced. Democracy, therefore, can only work if such conditions are met.

Besides these peculiarities, in many electoral laws of different countries we encounter several other "inventions," reflecting the à-la-carte "democratic" preferences of party leaderships. In Germany, for example, half of the members of parliament are elected from a list of candidates arranged by the leadership of each party, while the other half compete in the election process to win in single-seat constituencies, as is the case in the election of all representative seats in the USA, where the winner takes all. This means, especially for the US system, that, theoretically, half of the US population may have no representation whatsoever in Congress in some of the regions – and yet this is still called a democratic system. In the US, the electoral law does not prescribe an electoral threshold. It does something worse. All electoral districts, be they for representatives or senators, are of the single-seat type for representatives, with two seats in each state for the senators, where the winner takes all. It is no wonder that only two significant parties have been operating in the USA since time immemorial. That also is called a democracy.

To follow from the above, we may also ask which type of government system should be used, the parliamentarian system or the presidential one? The presidential system of government does not face problems associated with the formation of government, whereas the parliamentarian system, as we have seen above, does. However, the presidential system encounters other issues, which arise when, in the US, for example, the House of Representatives or the Senate is controlled by the President's opposition party. The President is then faced with a serious problem if he or she cannot find ways of coming to some agreement with the opposition.

**Coming back to the case of Greece, the electoral law proposed for the time being, should be one of simple proportional representation. The law also provides a bonus, at least for the foreseeable future, of additional parliamentary seats, which works as an incentive for parties to form a coalition government that has a parliamentary majority even without the additional bonus seats. These seats are taken from the**

**parties that do not participate in the coalition government on a basis of proportionality, depending on their strength, and they are given, again on a proportional basis, to the parties of the coalition government. The electoral law should also have a low electoral threshold, at least for some time, for any party to enter parliament. This measure will keep the number of parties represented in parliament down to a minimum, ensuring, however, that there will always be more than two.**

The electoral law, as one can see, is a very important matter. It can make or break the democratic process. For this reason, the party leadership and law makers must keep in mind the following issues:

**Human nature.** Our nature automatically privileges personal interests, because these assume a higher priority than collective interests. For this reason, as I emphasized above, with regard to collective decisions and actions taken by a group or society, all members must benefit from the outcomes, and according to rules that have been previously defined and agreed upon. Democracy, therefore, can only work if these conditions are met.

**Public institutions**. The function of institutions in a democratic system cannot be bypassed by special groups operating outside the framework of the democratic process. The interests of special groups should be represented adequately and openly, in the same way as other interests are being represented within the institutions. Otherwise, there is a risk of undermining the performance of the democratic institutions. These practices, unfortunately, are carried out with the help of the political parties. As we have commented earlier, some political parties, especially the strongest, benefit from such practices, which have as a result the so-called demise of democracies.

**Transparency of information provided to the public.** In any kind of democracy, the people need to have access to relevant information. In ancient Athens, most of the information was shared in the assemblies. The agenda of the assemblies was circulated on wax tablets. We can therefore surmise that the Athenians knew how to read and write. Because of the need in democracies to have an informed public, phonetic script and the combination of letters into syllables were invented. These inventions would later be used by all Europeans to put their languages into writing. This was another contribution Athenian democracy made to the world.

Today, the information that reaches the public in any nation on this planet is interspersed with a large amount of propaganda, personal opinions, and fake news, broadcasted mainly by all sorts of rogue journalists on a daily basis, a privilege that other members of society do not enjoy. One might even ask the question: **Has truth become a fiction?** The result, which we call information, produces total confusion among the citizens of the world, not least through the help of the Internet. However, for democracy to work, and at least if we use elections for appointing all political public officials, we need to effect major changes in this area.

In a democratic system, the public must have access to all information produced by all parties that are represented in parliament. Therefore, all existing sources of information should be openly available. In this way, people will know what each party stands for on all the issues that concern the living standards in that society. Firstly, and most importantly, all the news sources must report all the discussions that take place in parliament. The key point in all this, is for the public to know the positions of each party and how each party votes in each case. Any **commentary** by the so-called rogue journalists, as it is presented today, is of no use to the public. If any journalists want to comment, they should join the party of their choice or form their own party if they prefer. Democracy offers equal opportunities to all its citizens, including journalists, but not only to the latter, as is often the case today. The appropriate forum for commentary of this sort should be the parliament, where all the different positions and political currents are represented.

The situation in this area today is the worst possible one. Under such conditions, democracy cannot work. Many of the existing media belong to private interests. Aside from how good or bad is the quality of the information they propagate, which, in many cases, may be far from what citizens in a democratic society would expect to read or hear, these private centers of information are the only ones, from among all the citizens in a society, to have this particular privilege of bombarding the public with all kinds of information. This violates an important axiomatic principle which concerns the equal rights of every citizen. And what is more disturbing, is that the people are asked to pay for all this information, even though they never asked for it, including the profits the private centers are making. In fact, the hidden cost of this information, which some providers pretend to deliver free of charge, is far higher than we may think, and all of it is paid by the citizens, who are also required to pay higher prices for any products that are being advertised in the media. The companies producing these commodities add the cost of advertising to the retail price.

This situation has further negative side-effects. Products of multinational corporations, which have more money for advertising, eventually edge out of the market-shelves other products that are produced by smaller local firms which are unable to compete against those giant multinational corporations.

Another negative side-effect is that the entire, and vital, development program of any smaller country will be impaired in the long run, and eventually it may even be derailed.

The media in Greece try to convince the public that their services are free of charge. However, licenses for TV stations in Greece are sold at public auctions; the cheapest one was sold last year to a private owner for a sum of over €50 million. We may then ask an obvious question: Did the owner spend €50 million to provide the citizens information at no cost? That is very hard to believe. All these networks are very well organized worldwide, and as they currently operate, they represent a major obstacle to the good functioning of democracies. Along with this process, we also have the claim that all this mendacious and propagandistic information is produced by the politicians themselves. There is no doubt that there are politicians who are involved in the schemes of these networks; however, the deed is not done by politicians who want to serve democracy, but rather by politicians who are in the employment of these huge centers that want to control information for their own purposes. We know that democracy needs other tools in order to work properly.

Any citizen in a democracy should be informed through sources of known political affiliation, party journalists, not rogues of unknown identity. The public of a civic society should receive daily news through all media from every political party, large or small, as regards their positions on all matters concerning welfare, security, and the future of the members of society. It is because of this information that they should go to the ballot box. Information provided on this basis will also spare us the ordeal we all suffer from the countless advertisements on TV and radio for all the different products, some of which are useless, and even repulsive. Unfortunately, like so many other things, technology, too, instead of serving society, is used to promote interests alien to the concerns of its members. As far as contributing towards the improvement of the cultural level of the members of society is concerned, little emphasis is placed on it. The only content that passes through is what the market dictates.

Political parties that reach a certain percentage of the votes should be funded by tax money and not through private donations, which should be prohibited by law for all political parties, irrespective of size. People should understand that this is also the cheapest way by which we obtain the best and most important outcome: we get a democratic result, and we know at the same time how and how much money is spent by each party. We should never forget that eventually the private funding of parties becomes the people's expense in the long run, only in this latter case the cost for the taxpayers is even greater.

If all the above points are observed to protect and assist the democratic process, we can be sure that democracy will begin to operate more appropriately. However, most of the above wouldn't be required if the political parties had proceeded to reforms like the ones proposed in this book in the first place. But the efforts do not stop here. Some further measures, requiring additional constitutional adjustments, will be developed in the following chapters.

We should not forget that from the time of **Solon** to the reforms of **Cleisthenes** a period of almost a century went by, and between the time of **Cleisthenes** and the reforms of **Ephialtes,** there were another fifty years. Social and political changes need their time to mature. In those days, the time pressure for major social changes was not as high. Today, however, we do not have much time because of the adverse environmental developments, especially the melting of the arctic ice, and the provocative way wealth is being distributed. The political system that has brought us to this point must change. The solution to the major problems that are threatening life on this planet can be delivered only by a true democracy.

# Chapter Four

**4.1 Strengthening Existing Democracies Through Reforms**

The proposal made for electing the leaders of a political party, and the model for drawing up the list of party candidates for parliament, and for determining after the elections the specific candidates who will become members of parliament, can be applied to both regional or state and local (though not national) government and for all types of government. The example we will look at is local government in Greece, especially with respect to its operationality, and we will then identify further reforms that are needed for its improvement, in order to transform it into a democratic local government. Some reforms may require constitutional changes. This will depend on the type of provisions that exist in the different constitutions concerning local government. The model for regional or state (though not national) government can be constructed by using the same procedure to elect the head of its governing and legislative body, in the same way as that proposed for electing the leader of a party and for the selection of parliamentary candidates. At the end of the chapter we will seek to propose a new type of central government which will operate democratically. The aim of the proposed models is to make existing pressure groups of any kinds redundant. The proposed models enhance the role of all legislative bodies, in which the representation of the people now becomes a reality. With all these reforms democracy, at very long last, comes to the foreground, and the welfare of the people will finally be the primary focus.

## 4.2 Local Government

In Western-style democracies, local government is constructed as a miniature copy of central government. Local government provides services and goods in most areas where the central government does too. Local government can also impose its own taxes. The only areas where local government is not involved are defense and foreign affairs, even though local government does get involved in the area of foreign affairs to some extent, by building relations with other local governments abroad. As a result, we see in local government the same symptoms of mismanagement of funds and personnel due to incompetence, and the unlawful practices of some elected officials, which is paradoxical, if we consider that devolution is done in the name of strengthening the institutions of democracy. The matter gets even worse through the policies of some countries to push towards ever larger municipalities under local government. The argument made by the proponents of such policies is that the bigger the municipality, the better the chances for it to be economically viable. Designing municipalities exclusively as economic units is a perspective that misses the point. Politics should come first when what is at stake is the smooth running of democracy. This means people's participation.

Larger municipalities might also mean that more funds are available to the city halls for additional mismanagement and bribes. The more money there is available, the higher the potential for corruption. Yet the mismanagement of funds and human resources is only one aspect. What is more upsetting is the issue of the obstruction of the democratic process that is caused by these terrible artificial constructs, when, in the name of better prospects of economic viability for the municipality, more and more villages around large cities are absorbed within the same administrative district, increasing the distance between the citizens and their natural local leaders. In this sense, these developments can be seen as the gravediggers of democracy. The tragic consequence is to see beautiful villages turning into ghost towns, while the urban centers at the same time see their population numbers exploding, thus leading to a further decrease in the quality of life in the cities. Today, cities all over the world are turning into human jungles, where crime and drug use are thriving. This process should be reversed for democracy to be able to work, for all the good reasons mentioned above.

The Oxford Professor Paul Collier, in his book *The Future of Capitalism* (12, p. 7) describes, with some sadness, similar events in his birthplace in

England "I have lived the new geographic divide between booming metropolis and broken provincial cities. My hometown of Sheffield [is] the emblematic broken city ... I have lived the divide in skills and morale, between super-successful families and families disintegrating into poverty..." There are thousands, and more, such stories of tragedy. All these stories are, quite simply, the work of the capitalist model of production, which so inspired the socialist party of Greece, that it went ahead with a reform program for local government called Kapodistrias. This accelerated the abandoning of villages by the young, who were seeing their hopes for adequate living standards disappearing from their homelands. Another "genius" came along next, who further aggravated matters with another program of reforms called Callicrates, which made conditions even worse than they were. These reforms totally wiped out whatever democratic nuances might have existed.

To begin with, local government is precisely where some form of direct democracy can be applied more easily, and more successfully, than in any other area of government, and this is true especially in the villages, where populations are small. In large cities, we could think of smaller units (neighborhoods that would be smaller than boroughs) where direct democracy can be applied; subsequently, all the small tesserae can be assembled, as one does in a mosaic, to make up the whole city. The smaller the tesserae, the better this system works. We might well ask whether it is possible to find a sufficient number of competent people to run all these local councils, when it is even hard to elect mayors for our cities, who are competent enough to deal with the complexity of today's problems. The same reservation applies to presidents or prime ministers of countries, and these concerns are not far from the truth. Indeed, today's democracies tend to elect the wrong persons for the job, regardless of whether they are merely incompetent or just plain criminal. The more à la carte democracies there are, the greater this danger becomes. If we were to implement the kind of democracy this proposal is trying to build, these errors would be considerably reduced, without of course disappearing entirely. This is because the new model anticipates the use of independent implementation organizations, which are run by specialists elected by the local legislative bodies and are under the strict scrutiny of the latter. Even then, however, democratic structures can be used to bring about undesirable results, the reasons for which are to be found in the infamous intrinsic nature of human beings.

Both in local or regional and central governments, an important issue in need of attention is the efficient utilization of funds and human resources. Both these areas require the work of specialists and a proper form of organization. Unfortunate electoral results, and the general way of organizing and running most countries today, have led to a squandering of funds and the mismanagement of human resources. These are the first casualties, which may result in cases where incompetent people are elected to leading positions, such as mayors and councilors, to whom the law entrusts the task of running municipal affairs. Other losses are incurred when local officials flaunt the laws and join organized crime to mismanage and essentially steal municipal funds, as we have seen happen in places all around the world.

In ancient Athenian democracy, experts were elected by the citizens' assembly to implement all decisions taken by the city-state. These experts were under the strict scrutiny of the assembly. Today, in line with this ancient thinking, we could organize all municipal affairs in such a way as to divide the single center of authority we have today into two. The first would consist of the elected mayor and the councilors, who constitute the local legislative assembly, and which would serve as the top authority. The second would be an independent authority, which would consist of a network of specialist departments, charged with the task of providing experts to the first authority to help them generate full and integrated plans for the development of the city. Later, this second body will shoulder the responsibility of implementing the final decisions taken by the local assembly. Integrated planning covers the whole spectrum of municipal services, and the setting up of infrastructure (building streets, schools, hospitals, etc.). For this reason, in each area there needs to be a broad range of independent authorities in operation, in order to provide all the services and commodities required by the city hall authorities.

In this new operational scheme, the funds required for planning and implementing the approved programs would go directly to the expert implementation bodies, which will be totally independent, and not part of the mayoral offices. The steps of implementation of the approved programs will be scrutinized by the local assembly based on the schedules and budgets agreed. In certain cases, the authority for planning and implementation can also serve more than one municipality.

Appointment to the local assembly will follow similar steps to those presented in Chapter Three regarding the formation of a party's political structures.

More specifically, each party will **elect** a candidate for the mayorship locally, using a procedure like that used in electing the leader of the party. The members of the party and the members of the local party structures, which have been selected by sortition, will be electing a mayoral candidate following the same procedure used for electing the party leader. The idea is to elect party officers, such as the leader of the party or the party candidate for mayor (and why not the party's presidential candidate in the USA?), using the procedure employed in the ancient Athenian democracy to elect experts, where all the voters in the relative assemblies are selected by sortition and are free of any collusion. Such assemblies are the local constituencies of a party (where the administrative body of the local organization is selected by sortition), and the regional assemblies (where all voters are free of collusion because they were all selected by sortition and for one term only).

The candidates for councilor appointments on the party's mayoral list, will be **selected**, in each party, in the same way as that developed in Chapter Three regarding the drawing-up of the party's list of parliamentary candidates, namely by double sortition. The first sortition is used to form the party list. All volunteers wishing to be city councilors are selected by sortition from the pool of candidates who are also members of the Development Councils of the party. The method of sortition is applied to each subsection of human endeavor, such as education, health, etc., in order to obtain an appropriate representation of the local citizens on the list and covering different specializations. A second sortition is used immediately after the mayoral elections are held, in order to determine the ranking of each candidate on the list. Depending now on each party's strength (the number of votes won), the specific elected councilors will be those determined by their ranking on the list. The local mayoral assembly can now be formed; it will consist of the mayor, the leading candidates on the lists of parties that have passed the electoral threshold for local government and have received enough votes for the election of at least one councilor, and all the other elected councilors. This kind of local assembly will have many of the characteristics of the sessions held by the ancient Athenian parliament, and it is the best that can be achieved under current conditions today. Improvements may be needed, but these can only come after this system has been tried and tested for some time. The tenure of each party's mayoral candidate may be renewed once, and the tenure of a party's elected councilors may extend to one term only. The elected mayor can renew his candidacy for one additional term.

In local elections today, we also have the so-called independent candidates. My scheme has no place for independent candidates, as such a feature would allow the old system to re-enter through the back door. However, it does not exclude the possibility of local parties being formed on the same basis as national parties. Class struggle exists not only on a national basis; it is equally active on a local basis. We need procedures that are transparent for societies, and the proposed use of sortition ensures just that.

The proposed new form of local government provides:

1. A more effective control mechanism (the city council), which is local, and whose members are elected for a single term through procedures that take out of the picture collusion and corruption precisely at the level where it is known what decisions are to be implemented and when a task will be completed. The benefits of this mechanism, namely an assembly (the city council) which has in a way been selected by sortition, will be most evident when projects are completed on schedule and within budget. The officials of the municipal assembly will be able to show the finished project to the people. The credit generated will also be passed on to the political parties involved. In cases where the planned work has not been completed in time by the new independent implementation organizations, the blame will not be passed on to the parties involved. There will be no political repercussions for the elected mayor and the city councilors. The people will know this, because they participate in the control mechanism through the parties.

2. A new way of operating, whereby it is easier to control and inspect an independent implementation organization, than it is to check on elected officials. In today's way of organization, the first excuse the municipal officials will put forward is that the control exerted on them is politically motivated, thus complaining about political persecution.

3. An appropriate organizational structure, offering the people greater prospects that any required works will be carried out according to sufficient standards.

4. Urgently needed funds and human resources will be utilized more efficiently. The independent implementation organizations will no longer be run by elected officials, but by professional managers and

experts. Parties will not select the personnel for these organizations, as this will no longer be their job. The hiring will be decided by managers in charge of these organizations, using proper criteria specified by law for each position to be filled.

5. A new model of operation for all types of media in the area, along the lines sketched out in Chapter Three, will provide all the necessary information to the people, giving them better knowledge about what needs to be done and in what order, thus enhancing the functionality of the control mechanisms.

A very important positive consequence of this way of running local government affairs is that it will sever the umbilical cord that exists today between all elected officials (mayors etc.) and municipal employees, as well as voters, who tend to band together for mutual "benefits" which will be enjoyed not by all, but only by the select few. Local development also gets a better treatment, achieving higher standards, free of mismanagement and corruption. Such development can or should be promoted by local establishments, private or public, thus bolstering local economy and employment. The entire nation's productivity will grow thanks to the new model of operation, making more funds available as less mismanagement occurs. The implementation of all decisions is carried out by implementation organizations run by experts. In such a context, Paul Collier's suggestions will have much better chances of being implemented and allowed to produce results in the business sector, where now the capitalist model of production will acquire also cultural components, which will transform the economic man into a cultured fellow-man: we will thus be able to see a real transformation of the capitalist model of production into the model Adam Smith was dreaming of.

## 4.3 Regional or Central Government

If the reforms suggested here regarding political parties and local government are applied, the actual running of democracy will improve in an impressive way – even if the media continue to work as they do today. This assertion is based, of course, on the assumption that sortition will be implemented in key areas of party organization and local government. The application of sortition will ensure the selection of all public officials, except party leaders and mayors, through the use of lots and for a single term, rather than through any kind of elections, where the promotion of specific candidates is decided by party bosses, pressure groups of various kinds, and powerful centers of influence (some of which operate through the media). Furthermore, due to the use of sortition, the party leaders and mayors will be significantly less powerful but more competent, even in the respective legislative bodies where membership will no longer be the result of choices made by party leaders or mayors, but the outcome of a two-tiered sortition process. Some people may believe that under the current system they are personally electing the members of parliament, but it is an open secret to most of us that this no longer holds true. However, what is proposed in this book does not, on the one hand, deprive people of their right to vote for their president or their prime minister, and their governor or mayor, while at the same time retaining a true potential to reverse the way things stand today, when not even half of the eligible voters are going to the polls, because they no longer believe that their vote will make any difference.

Assuming now that all the reforms proposed above take place, can we be certain that democracy will eventually work for all? As we stated above, democracy must work for all, poor and rich. The answer to this question is that democracy will now work for more people, but still not for all. For this to happen, people must be willing to undertake some additional reforms to increase the authority of parliament and change the role of the executive power, the cabinet.

With this new synthesis, which includes MPs from all social backgrounds and every region of the nation (as has been ensured using a two-tiered sortition), parliament receives more power than before. Being a member of parliament now comes much closer to the meaning of being a true representative of the people who belong to one's social background or geographical region, and MPs will be in a stronger position to represent the interests of the people they speak for. Parliamentarians are no longer fettered by the shackles of the past. Their presence in parliament is not due to their party leader or any other centers of influence inside or outside the party. It is only a matter of luck, as well as of the percentage a party secures in the election, while the MPs' term in parliament ends with the coming of the next election. Thus, the personal ambitions of parliamentarians will not be boosted by any outside centers of influence. The only remaining bond is with their respective party. Will they betray the people in their region for the benefit of some distant party ambitions? There may be some who will, but there will be more who will refuse to do so. In ancient Athens, the same was the case for the political officials, selected by sortition, as well as the male voters in the citizens' assembly over the age of twenty, and the result was that the majority would not abuse their position in favor of ancillary interests. In view of these results, we may assume that the same will happen today.

What else might there be that could go wrong? The only remaining danger that one might think of is that of politicians being bought. This does indeed happen today, but the proposed reforms will make the practice of bribery far too expensive, for now the bribe giver must pay much more and buy the services of a much larger number of individuals. Through the proposed reforms we manage to transform parliament into an assembly far better than the one in the ancient democracy of the Athenians, and much better than the ancient parliament. Its social and geographical synthesis will now be far superior, especially if we extend these measures further, to include to some additional reforms concerning the powers of the cabinet members.

Prime ministers and cabinet members have certain powers which, when exercised, can throw a spanner into the works of the democratic process. It is well known that parties address themselves to certain social groups according to their ideological perspective. These social groups are their clients, something the party leaders do not forget, especially if they are seeking reelection for another term. This favoritism is evinced in many areas, but the preferred method is the increase in salaries and pensions, as well as the appointment of people to the civil service, where they enjoy job security for life. Interventions like these ensure many votes, but they also create injustices and unequal treatment of the citizens as a result. This is where democracy does not work for everyone, and therefore all such powers must be abolished. Some must be transferred to the independent implementation organizations proposed above, while many others need to be placed under the jurisdiction of parliament.

Such additional reforms will transform the now powerful cabinet into a body whose role will resemble that of the 50 MPs that each tribe in the democracy of ancient Athens delegated for one year. Between sessions, these were in charge of overseeing the work carried out by the experts and were also preparing the agenda and putting together proposals for the next sessions of the citizens' assembly. Once such a different framework has been developed, it is time for changes in the composition of the cabinet. This should be the result of an election in parliament to select the prime minister or head of cabinet, through a succession of two votes, where the second round will decide between the two strongest candidates. With a similar process, the rest of the cabinet members should also be elected. The cabinet must consist only of parliamentarians, because the experts who are also elected by parliament to lead the independent implementation organizations are not MPs themselves. At this point, the law of proportional representation must be freed from provisions of any kind, for they will not be needed anymore. The country will always have a prime minister and a cabinet. The institution of the president of the republic or the monarch is no longer needed and must be abolished.

Today we have an executive power, just as we have an executive power in local government, which, after the elections, should implement a program that was promised to the people, since it was through the people's vote that the party or parties won the election. That is why certain reforms are necessary to ensure that the executive power will acquire its new proper function. Let us state some of them:

1. The umbilical cord between prime ministers, ministers and all the different secretaries who constitute the executive power of the party or parties in power, **and** all civil servants, should be severed. One way this can be done is to remove, once and for all, the power of the executive branch to negotiate matters such as salaries, pensions, etc. with non-governmental organizations and pressure groups of any kind (unions etc.). All people working in government, and all those working in the private sector in similar positions, should enjoy the same benefits. Privileges such as permanent jobs, for example, and other perks handed out for the purpose of getting in return the votes of the civil servants in the coming elections, need to be abolished. The bill for all these expenses is paid by the taxpayers, and only they should have the authority to approve or disapprove such items through plebiscites or other appropriate methods. One important rule in a democratic country is that all citizens have equal rights and should be treated equally. If this is the case, special groups outside the framework of the democratic process will not be able to override its institutional safeguards. The interests of special groups should be represented adequately and transparently within the institutions, just as other interests are being represented. Otherwise, there is a risk that

the functioning of the democratic institutions may be undermined, and often this does transpire with the help of political parties that benefit from such interventions, resulting in a subversion of the democratic process.

### What are the actual damages to democracy?

To begin with, this special relation of the executive power with those employed in the civil service is highly unethical. As we can see in many places on this planet, this relation leads to certain members of society being treated differently and receiving different remuneration for the same or similar work. In addition, since this special treatment increases the expenses as the body of civil servants grows, the burden on the budget also increases, to which all the taxpayers are obliged to contribute.

The financial resources needed to pay the salaries of the civil servants are basically produced in the private sector and through certain public activities, if they are run efficiently; these are the only activities where most of the wealth is being produced. Most other sectors, for better or worse, consume this wealth. When the expenses for the civil service, tax evasion, and unlimited profiteering get out of hand, an economic crisis knocks on the door. This is when production of wealth is being surpassed by the outflows in the public sector, and/or in the rates of capital income, and/or in the area of tax evasion. These conditions set in motion the most dangerous forces, producing unemployment in the private industry, an increase in taxes, cuts in pensions, and a further contraction of the wealth produced, triggering a vicious spiral of tax increases, further cuts in pensions, further increases in unemployment, and the further increase of public debt. And the icing on the cake is the civil service – tyrannizing the rest of society, wanting to keep its hard-won privileges.

2. The executive power, that is the ruling party or parties, should **only** have the authority to **oversee** the ongoing execution of parliament-approved programs by the appropriate independent implementation authority or authorities. The executive power must not be allowed to manage these independent authorities. As things stand today, in most cases we see how cabinet members take on the management of the relevant bureaucracy and try to "implement" their own private agendas. In most cases, cabinet members are not the most able and

knowledgeable people to manage such vast disparate groups left over by the previous cabinet, whether their own, or belonging to the previous opposition government. Each of these ministers may even try to transform the bureaucracy into something akin to a party constituency, or even worse, their personal private entity, and, in the end, the implementation of the government program will not be pursued. Instead, many political favors will be exchanged ahead of the minister's and the party's reelection. I've seen even a labor minister doubling workers' minimum wages overnight, thus throwing out of the window any traces of competitiveness that the economy had achieved.

3.   Hiring, especially in the public sector, must not be left to the executive power either. The political favors granted by cabinet members, especially when a particular minister stays in the same post for several years, can create a curious result, where we see a characteristic mix of employees in the department, the vast majority of whom, by some strange coincidence, hail from the minister's constituency. Again, the payoff is the reelection of the minister, and not only. In this way, civil servants with even rudimentary capabilities will be few and far between. The system of political favors within a government department operates day and night, top to bottom. To avoid these occurrences, all hiring in the public sector should be done by the appropriate independent implementation authorities, provisions for which have been made in the constitution through further amendments. In this way, any conflict of interests is left out, and the public sector does not grow uncontrollably. Requirements in human resources must only be determined by the officials running the independent implementation authorities. In certain countries, these conditions are being satisfied in some way, and a degree of progress can be seen there, which confirms the incremental benefit of this way of hiring personnel for society. The better organized these independent implementation authorities are, the greater will be the benefit for society.

4.   An independent authority that operates within the framework of the national parliament should be in place, to monitor continuously the progress of net economic growth, which should be greater or equal to the expenses in the public sector, plus the losses due to tax evasion and the rate of capital gain after imports have hopefully been offset

by exports. Otherwise, these too enter the equation. The importance of continuous monitoring can be understood if we consider that the sum of a year's spending produces the revenue for the following year's budget, which comes from income tax and VAT (Value Added Tax), plus revenue that comes mainly from interest and land taxation. This latter part of the budget is small compared to what is needed for the budget; the majority must come from the production of wealth in the private sector. When the private sector starts shrinking, public borrowing enters the picture, which over time may lead to the bankruptcy of entire countries.

5.  Besides eradicating or at least reducing everywhere the squandering of monetary and human resources, our model for an effective and just democratic system also aims at eliminating sources of financial fraud created by the executive power or the bureaucracy of the civil service through "convenient" legislation, which includes implicating "parliament" in these criminal processes. One such source is the invention of the **VALUE ADDED TAX (VAT, an invention of the European Union that was applied in Greece in 1986 for the purpose of satisfying the Sixth Directive of the EU. VAT replaced a different tax which was paid by the firms based on their annual turnover).**

Assuming that all the reforms proposed up to this point can be implemented, can we claim that the sessions of this new type of parliament will be closer to direct democracy than those of the assembly in ancient Athenian democracy, where participation was at times very poor and of low quality? This question is not without merit, for in the new parliament 100% participation of the parliamentarians, as the true representatives of their constituency on a national level, is ensured, whereas in the ancient assembly participation was effectively limited on many occasions to one or two thousand citizens, the majority of them coming from the city of Athens. Out of the ca. 20 to 45 thousand eligible voters, many thousands were absent with valid excuse. Which of the two legislative bodies may be considered the more scrupulous one from the perspective of their respective levels of participation? Obviously, the new type of legislative body is superior to the ancient model, for it employs voters of higher qualitative standards compared to those in the ancient legislative body. Most importantly, they are all of them collusion free.

## 4.4 Steps Towards an Acceptable Model for Democracy

Considering the explanations and arguments developed so far, we can now propose an appropriate model of democracy for our times. It appears that the ancient Greeks had studied human nature thoroughly, and invented a system, democracy, not for the purpose of changing the nature of man – which cannot be changed – but to offer human beings an alternative way, a way of fulfilling their dreams without preventing their fellow citizens from realizing their own goals as well. The time has now come for us to develop an urgently needed model that is appropriate for our democracy.

Attempts to bribe voters might still happen under our model for today's democracy as well, but they are likely to be very limited because of each voter's individual qualities in the assembly. Thus, those who seek to bribe their way to a position of power, may no longer be inclined to do so, for they may now have to bribe many more than just the leadership of a party, for instance, which could raise the cost of such inducements to quite high levels. Actually, there are a few records from ancient Athens of bribes being offered by the rich to unemployed citizens rather than to political officials, such as those offered by a wealthy politician named Kimon, an event that forced Pericles to pass a legal provision in the assembly which for the first time allowed the payment of stipends to members of parliament.

If we intend to recreate quality standards similar to or better than those that existed in ancient Athenian democracy, such as, for example, the distinctive conditions that will allow democracies to work in a parliamentarian type of assembly, certain important reforms must be made, starting with the way political parties operate. These reforms, which have been mentioned earlier, can be summarized as follows:

1. All party functionaries wishing to hold political positions of any level within the party, and who are selected today by vote, should be selected by sortition, provided they meet the required criteria for the job. Tenure should be limited to one term, which may last, at least for the time being, for a maximum of four years (to ensure a change and continuity of experience one renewal of term of 25% of the legislators by sortation is considered harmless).

2. The party list of parliamentary candidates is similarly drawn up by sortition, using the process explained above. The electoral process is limited to voting for the party, and not for individual candidates. After

the election a second round of sortition will determine the ranking of each candidate on the electoral list.

3.  No single-seat constituencies should be allowed anymore, while the electoral law should be that of simple proportional representation, with an added clause requiring that all parties reach a minimum percentage of votes, as specified by the relative electoral law, in order for them to delegate members to parliament. This provision is included in the law, as an interim measure, in order to avoid the proliferation of small political parties.

4.  The executive power assumes the role that the Athenian parliament had in ancient Greece, and more precisely the role of the council of the prytaneis (highest city magistrates), which consisted of 50 parliament members from each tribe. The implementation of policies and development programs decided by the parliament is assigned to independent organizations working under the supervision of parliament, to which they must report. The daily monitoring of all the implementation organizations is done by what is today called the executive power, making sure that the implementation organizations are fulfilling their tasks according to schedule.

5.  The party leaders are elected in party assemblies by the party members who are now free of collusion, and these are held in every region across the country. In these regional congresses those who participate are the members of regional party structures, who are determined through sortition, and any additional regional party members deemed necessary, who are selected also by sortition. Candidates for the party presidency will be invited to speak at these regional congresses, thus giving voters an opportunity to form an educated opinion about each candidate. It must be stressed here that wherever voting takes place, those in the assembly, who are called to select the president of the party, its mayoral candidate, and experts, or nonpolitical officials, are all selected by sortition and for one term. Those voters must represent the whole spectrum of the region's distinctive attributes. For example, if the Electoral College in each state in the US were selected from among the party members by sortition, then the candidates for the presidency would have to be able to demonstrate in each state assembly that they are qualified to run as candidates for the US presidency. This kind of

procedure is also much more economical for the public than any other. We should not forget that any kind of electoral expense, no matter where it comes from, is being born in the end by the public.

6. The candidates for the presidency of each party, and the parties themselves, are regularly given equal time or space in the media in order to publicize their views or programs. These expenses are covered by public funds. No financial support, or support of any other form, by the private sector is allowed.

It should not be assumed that the election process used for members of parliament or other politically related officials today provides us with the most able appointees; in many cases, it produces results of collusion or a dependency on centers of influence within the party or outside it. And no one should forget the benefits that ancient Athenian democracy bequeathed to humanity, using sortition instead of elections for selecting their single-term political officials. Today, as the environment faces critical threats, democracy remains the only alternative for its salvation.

## 4.5 Reforms in the Judiciary Sector

The last but by no means least important point regards the reforms that must be carried out in the judiciary sector, where we also need to achieve independence from the institutions of executive power, which is not the reality in any of the so-called democracies today, for all the protestations by the executive about judicial independence. In Greece, the executive, through the ministry of justice, selects and appoints the presiding judge for the Supreme Court, and the two highest justices of the peace for the District Courts. Through this process, party politics intrude upon the institution of justice. Beyond this constitutional provision, there are many other interventions by the executive power at lower levels in the same area, which we do not see, or become aware of, with the effect that all citizens do not receive equal treatment before the courts. In addition, we have a fully operative syndicalism at all the different levels, also opening the doors to party politics, and thus subverting the democratic principle that we are all equal before the law, which subsequently goes out the window. It is very important that all citizens feel that equal treatment is being ensured in all social environments and institutions. This is one of the basic principles of democracy. Without provisions for equal treatment and equal opportunities for citizens in a democracy, it is impossible to transform a society with the characteristics of a jungle, into a cultured society.

Before certain specific reforms are proposed for this area, we must also say a few words about what defines a court decision as just.

Every society has its own history and its traditions. These two domains determine many aspects of people's life, as well as their positions or their understanding of what is right or wrong in their daily dealings. Socrates, the ancient philosopher, used to say that what is just is also legal. This implies that something that is considered legal, is not necessarily also just. People expressing their views about court decisions often observe that some of these are not just, even though they may be in accordance with the law. This may happen because governments and parliaments on many occasions pass laws that are not just, or because judges can be far removed from social reality. However, it may happen that the majority in a society, experiencing repeatedly, and year after year, the way that the executive power passes laws which may be constitutional but not just, gets so used to this kind of legislation, as to consider these legal provisions also to be just. Notorious examples of such cases are the electoral laws, the process of selecting political officers through elections, and many others. Furthermore, in a democratic country where the people have the first and the last word in all matters, even the institution of justice, similar to the other two fundamental powers (the executive and parliament), cannot be totally independent, but faces certain constraints which are related to society's overall sense of what is just or not. In other words, justice does not only involve theoretical matters, but it encompasses issues that have to do with all the questions we have explored so far. After all, the institution of the juror, or lay assessor, was invented based on such considerations, and those who undertake that role do not need to have special knowledge on matters of what is just and what is not. It is enough from them to be recruited, through sortition, from among those members of society who have a general sense of justice, which is why jurors at the time had to be over the age of 30. In modern Greece, the institution of jurors – even though it was an invention of their ancient forbearers in Athens – has been unfortunately almost eliminated. If the issue of justice were only a matter for the technocrats, then it would not be necessary to use judges either. We could just as well program all the laws into large computers and let them make all the decisions. Obviously, in one way or another, such constraining parameters are incorporated in the constitutions of any democratic country. As we said elsewhere, the three institutions, namely parliament, the executive, and the judiciary, constitute the foundations of a democratic country. We are committed to the existence of these foundations not as an end in itself, but as a means of guaranteeing the welfare of all, by bridling the barbarity of the members of a society, which is part of human nature, thus eventually elevating the cultural standards of a society.

On this basis, we can see why reforms must be undertaken in the area of justice, using criteria like those applied to the restructuring of the other two institutions of democracy, namely the use of sortition. Where and how sortition should be used depends to some extent on the processes used in different countries today. For these reasons, I will present the processes used in Greece today, and use them as a basis to propose some reforms that would lead to better days in this area elsewhere as well.

Today, for a Greek citizen to become a judge, he or she must have a university degree in law. Then, after graduation, he or she needs to have worked as a lawyer for two years in order to obtain a certain level of practical experience regarding the workings of the courts. After these two years, the lawyer must attend a university-level course where he or she acquires the knowledge required for being a judge. This part of the lawyer's training can take up to three years. Before being admitted to this course, they first must pass entrance examinations and meet certain additional requirements concerning the candidate's personality. All jurists who successfully complete the two- to three-year program are then hired as judges for life.

One step towards a reform of the judiciary would be to reassess the use of jurors on more occasions than is the case now, using sortition for their selection. In addition, judges trained through the process described above should have more than two years' practice as lawyers. We may propose a requirement of at least six years of legal practice before admission to the training course for judges. In any case, young judges should be at least thirty years old when beginning their career. A review committee exists which is selected by sortition, and which evaluates the files of each judge for the purpose of promotion, and this should remain as it is. The leadership of the Supreme Court, and the attorneys general (the public prosecutors at the Supreme Court) should be selected by sortition from among the highest body of judges, and the promotion of judges should not be based primarily on the criterion of the number of years in service.

This process will ensure the independence of most judges. However, as all institutions in a democracy are under the scrutiny of the people, parliament, which is the body where all the power of the people is concentrated, may also need to have top judges and attorneys under its scrutiny.

# Chapter Five

---

## 5.1 Democracy as a Means Towards Social Welfare

In the introduction to this book, the Greek financial debt crisis was mentioned as the instigation for my writing it. At least one cause for this crisis must certainly be attributed to the continuous mismanagement of public affairs by most public officials, a state which had been going on for years. This was primarily due to the ineffective organization of the state's infrastructure, which allowed the squandering of all kinds of resources. This infrastructure, moreover, had been developed through all types of collusion between elected officials and voters or bribe givers. Another cause for this financial crisis must be attributed to the capitalist model of production, whereby the accumulation of capital had systematically exceeded the rate of production and revenue. Both reasons are primarily the result of the two World Wars in the twentieth century, which have had devastating consequences, and which also led to a catastrophic civil war, and subsequently to a dictatorship imposed by the secret services of the USA. It had the blessing of the "democratic" US government, which used the Greek armed forces (which were well under the control of these secret services at the time) for as long as was necessary. The time required, in fact, was the time it took for the preparation and implementation of the Turkish invasion of Cyprus.

Greek history, since the war of independence in 1821, and to our days, has exhibited throughout the characteristics of a Greek tragedy. The above circumstances, which arose because democracy was absent, are responsible for this extraordinary misfortune that has befallen Greece. However, even today, one of them is still very much with us, and is in fact deeply rooted in most so-cieties around the world, and that is the capitalist model of production. It operates today globally, using the West as its primary base, where, presumably, democracy is the working model, with ever more capital and means at its disposal. Such wealth is the fruit of unregulated capitalist models of production, which will make matters more difficult for the future, unless real democracy comes to the rescue across the continents, especially in the so-called democracies of the Western world.

By now, more and more people and organizations have realized that the globalization of the markets, and the organization of production chains or the provision of services by the multinationals have prompted a whole spectrum of significant unethical conduct in these corporations, including total tax avoidance or the unjust distribution of created wealth: high rates of accumulated capital, very high revenues and bonuses for managing personnel, as compared to the rest of the workforce, and many other unethical practices which are related to the corruption of elected officials and of civil servants on a global scale.

Until today, the United Nations (UN), and numerous non-governmental organizations created for the purpose of somehow breaking down the activities of the multinationals and of certain so-called safe-haven countries, have not been successful in their efforts to achieve a fairer distribution of created wealth and to stop this unregulated rally for money that has resulted in the continuous increase of accumulated capital as compared to production, labor income increases, and a high rate of unemployment.

A significant contribution to the UN's failure was certainly the great influence that some large countries exert over many smaller nations around the globe, thus providing, through their official and "unofficial" activities, the necessary cover-up for the operations of big capital.

The UN's principles for a worldwide agreement, as well as its directives for Economic Cooperation and Development, which demand the application of universal (**multicultural**) ethical and cultural values, have not brought the desired results. The Social and Economic Council of the United Nations, which was set up by the Secretary General of the UN Kofi Annan in 1999 with the objective of improving the just distribution of created wealth, has not been able to inspire corporations around the globe to join its efforts to any great extent. By 2010, only 5,200 firms from 130 countries had joined the effort to make their business operations more ethical. The principles of the Economic

Council concern the promotion of ethical conduct in various corporations worldwide. They advocate respect for human rights, responsible monitoring of working conditions within the firms, respect and preventive protection of the environment, and action against corruption of all forms. The efforts of the Economic Council will not be able to bring the expected results if democracy is absent around the globe.

In 1993, a Declaration of Global Ethics was circulated in Chicago, which was voted by the Parliament of the World's Religions. This Manifesto for Global Economic Ethics (42) accepts market rules and competition and has as its objective to place the implementation of these rules on a solid ethical basis for the good of all. In his foreword to the publication of the manifesto, Jeffrey Sachs, director of the Earth Institute at Columbia University, and special advisor to the Secretary General of the UN on its Millennium Development Goals, defined global economic ethics as an important step in the direction of viable economic development. He referred to the position of the philosopher and academic Hans Küng, one of the proponents of the manifesto, that globalization cannot succeed without being based on the right ethics, and on cultured societies around the globe. He also states that problems such as hunger, which is responsible for the death of millions of children every year, diseases, etc., are not due to a lack of resources, but are the outcome of a lack of ethical conduct by the usual suspects. The Parliament of the World's Religions, and the distinguished professors Jeffrey Sachs and Hans Küng, must realize that cultured societies cannot be produced by what are, at best, oligarchic systems of government, and which plague the entire world, where the motto of the economic man is every man for himself.

**Cultured societies can be produced only by real democracies.**
The Manifesto for Global Ethics, which demands and expects ethical conduct from the multinationals, is an important wakeup call for these companies; yet how can we expect practical results to come out of a group that is responsible for existing conditions worldwide? I am afraid I still need to be convinced. We know now that without true democracies, one can never expect cultured societies to develop. The manifesto reminds us of a famous popular saying that is an apt description of this situation: we have set the fox to guard the henhouse ... And if further proof were needed among the many cases cropping up in our days around the world, we can look at the experiment carried out

by Professor Klaus M. Leisinger, an expert in business ethics, who is President and Director of the Novartis Foundation for Continued Development: he was not even able to convince the managers of Novartis, a pharmaceutical corporation, to apply ethical conduct to their business activities around the globe. The manifesto is certainly a very good document, but it is like putting the cart before the horse, for as long as the political conditions remain as they are, the nine individuals who today own as much wealth as the three billion poorest people (almost half of the planet's population), will increase their share of global wealth even further.

This type of behavior will continue to exist as long as the myth of the so-called "free" markets continues to have its ideological proponents, in addition to those who are simply making a living out of selling this myth, particularly those in charge of the big multinational corporations. In a way, the owners and managers of the multinationals remind me of the earthly representatives of whoever their respective god might be. The religion of the owners of the multinationals is their "free" market, through which they seek to save their golden "soul." The free market (without quotation marks) is certainly not the religion of the multinationals, for in such a market they may have to toil in order to survive, and with less money in their pockets. The "free" market, on the other hand, is certainly their religion, because they can also use the practices of corruption on a global scale in order to get wherever they wish to go. As an aside, theirs is the only religion that cultivates – with success, one might say – good relations with all other existing religions around the world.

At this point, it may be perhaps important to delve deeper into the concept of the free market. Adam Smith (43) had used it to underline the benefits that will accrue for the consumers, as regards product quality and lower prices, if such conditions, namely a free market, could exist and operate in a given region, local or national. No one would disagree that, if the products and services produced by companies were competing in a free market, then the benefits for the buyers would be tremendous. A free market is a mechanism which automatically promotes the sales of better and less expensive products. Also, in a free market every firm that produces commodities or offers services can participate and compete with other firms for the purpose of selling its products, and for the benefit of the people. This being so, the question then arises: can there be a free market at all? The answer to this question is not an easy one. Under the present political conditions, the free market exists only on paper, and not in real life, and given how the capitalist model of production operates, free markets cannot exist for pragmatic reasons. The claim made by some, that a free market can exist, is as true as the claim that there can be a physical process without any friction. What one can say at this point is that under a truly democratic process the capitalist model of production, through some effort, can be "refined," so that it may open the way to a free market. In other words, if a free market is to exist at all, then that market can only make its appearance in a truly democratic state.

The concept of the free market, which Adam Smith introduced in his seminal book *The Wealth of Nations*, and the concept of the citizens' assembly, which the ancient Athenians employed to promote direct democracy, go in parallel. Neither can the present market operate as a free market, nor can the citizens' assembly as it stands function democratically. In both areas, those who dominate the proceedings are the strong companies on the one side, and the powerful figures, which may also be supported by strong centers of interests, on the other. This means that other and different institutions must exist and operate than the present ones, before we can devise political instruments that will function in accordance with what they are designed for. The most important institution is a true democracy. It is this institution that will raise the citizens' cultural level in a society, which is a necessary condition for real changes to happen. **True democracy and cultured societies are the two necessary and sufficient, prerequisite conditions, which can contribute to the effort of devising the proper tools to ensure the flawless operation of the market and the democratic operation of a citizens' assembly with the right participants (who will be free of any collusion).** The just distribution of created wealth will ensue from these two processes.

In our days, the concept of globalization is also gaining prominence. There is considerable confusion, however, as to what globalization is all about. The same kind of confusion, even among some ideologists, existed as regards the historical phenomenon of imperialism. On the one side we have today those who consider globalization to be just an economic phenomenon. This position is promoted mainly by the proponents of the capitalist model of production, who claim that globalization benefits all people and all nations. There is, however, the other side, which claims quite the opposite. This side claims that globalization is a mechanism by which wealth is being transferred from the poorer nations to the rich ones. This argument is promoted mainly by

Marxists, and it sees the transfer as being essentially carried out from the poorer countries to the pockets of the rich. In addition, what we experience in wealthy nations is the transformation of large industrial areas into slumps and ghost towns, where unemployment and despair run high. As a result, we see a dangerous rise of extreme right-wing movements, which try to revive the eras of the regimes of Mussolini and Hitler. In between stand those who have mixed feelings about globalization.

Perhaps the best way to clear all confusion is for economists to study a model where the planet represents a global nation, and all existing nations represent companies which compete among themselves in order to sell their products in the market provided by the global nation. Aside from the macroeconomic study of the global nation, the economists should also study the microeconomics of the nation-companies, which now wear a different hat. In this way, they will be able to see what other constraints are involved in the economic productivity of each nation-company, such as the political, social and other conditions that enter into the picture, and how these conditions impair or assist the viability of these nation-companies. Then we will be able to see what globalization really produces, and for whom the bell tolls.

For one thing, the way one can come to some conclusion as to whether globalization is accomplishing its objectives is to examine its results. And the results tell us that in some poor countries, where multinationals have made investments because the wages were very low, and the taxes were likewise low or totally absent, thus providing the investors with higher profit margins, the income of the workers in these poor countries increased. On the other hand, however, the commodities produced by these multinationals in poorer countries, and as a result of globalization, started to replace local commodities produced in many rich countries, where salaries are much higher, therefore making local products more expensive, thus forcing the closing down of many companies, and causing the increase of unemployment in those areas.

It is interesting nonetheless to see what Pascal Lamy, who was in charge of the UN World Organization of Commerce, said in a speech in November 2019 to the students of the University of British Columbia, in Vancouver, Canada, about globalization, which is facing some problems of late. Among other things he said:

"My answer: in making globalization less painful, less stressing for humans and Nature, in being better at harnessing it than we have been recently. Starting

with focusing the right problem which is not globalization but capitalism [...
] And recognize that the present version of capitalism underlying globalization exacerbates its well-known flaws: instability, social injustice, environmental degradation." In order to deal with these problems, he proposed "a reform agenda around a few priorities: taming finance and its excesses, new systems to reduce social insecurity and cope with the digital revolution, turning production systems towards circularity through proper pricing of environmental externalities." With respect to the outcomes of globalization, these will depend on our competence to steer the dominant economic system, namely capitalism, towards a different direction. The report of the UN on Sustainable Development Goals provides the right picture as to where we should be heading. In any case, the reforms to the model of capitalism constitute the priority.

At this point, it may be of interest to look at the developmental path of the globalization of free trade and free capital movement, concerning primarily multinational corporations, since the accelerated beginnings of this process in the '70s, and until today. Soon after the start of the globalization of free trade that was promoted by the World Trade Organization on the basis of specific rules, we saw the appearance of regional trade agreements among countries popping up all over the globe, mainly as a reaction to the WTO's promotion of free trade. Whereas in the '80s only about seventy countries were participating in such regional trade agreement associations, their number soon skyrocketed to almost two hundred by the end of 2012. These developments should not be overlooked and must be explained on the grounds that the globalization of the free market did not work smoothly for all, especially after the Doha Development Round. Otherwise these countries would not have been on the lookout for better markets (essentially protected markets) for their products.

Today, with the trade war between the USA and China, we already witness the first signs of a rupture in the good working ties between Silicon Valley and China. The battle for the control of advanced technologies is gaining momentum each day, with the outcome being yet uncertain. It seems likely that the student is getting better than the teacher.

In any case, globalization is a very complex process, and no one can predict its outcome under the present conditions. For one thing, the international political circumstances are, and will be for a long time, very unstable. In this war between giants, it is not even possible to keep one's distance. The outcome of this fight will therefore affect everyone. Judging based on the millions of refugees crossing the national borders of wealthier countries, it is not hard to see what will happen. Erdogan to name one, a good friend of President Trump, is already using the refugees as a way of applying pressure on the European Union, while Erdogan's friend is raising walls to stop the invasion of millions of economic migrants. Does it or does it not look like a paradox? In fact, Erdogan has warned the Europeans that Europe's future will be, sooner or later, in the hands of Islamists, thus introducing religion already into the battlefield. That weapon may prove to be stronger than the various transactions involving advanced technologies that are being made through the regional trade agreements. After all, President Trump appeared to accept the use of such of weapons when he was declaring to the UN General Assembly that "the future belongs to patriots not globalists"!

Until then, we must see whether something might be available that can temper the effects of globalization. However, before we come to that, some clarifying comments are necessary regarding the nature of the sociopolitical processes, for some of the other proposals being put forward refer to them as being irreversible.

For example, Ulrich Beck (44), who proposes a formula for dealing with globalization, introduces the concept of the universality of all major issues in which humans are particularly interested and engaged, and which he considers to be irreversible processes. Perhaps it would be more appropriate to characterize these processes, associated with globalization or worldwide politics, as a one-way street, which can be crossed, however, in both directions, depending on the social conditions that apply in each case. Known historical data do not confirm any irreversible social processes. To begin with, irreversible processes are encountered exclusively in nature, and physical laws explain why they happen. In fact, all processes in nature are irreversible because of friction, which is manifested by the continuous increase of entropy associated with every physical process. Scientists, however, invent reversible (ideal) processes when they are interested to know only the relation between the initial and the final state of a system, and not the course through which the final state was attained. They can do this because they can use variables that are independent of the way in which one state of the system develops into another. When we study social processes, we are confronted with an entirely different situation. They are not like physical processes, and social friction is not like physical friction. **Social processes are explained by social laws, where social friction**

**works both ways. Depending on the type of social conditions that exist, the process can be any one of several types.** The economist Thomas Piketty, for example, found that, during the period from 1940 to 1980, the income of the richest ten percent in the USA, France, Germany, and the United Kingdom dropped by ten units compared to the Gross National Product (GNP). In the USA it went down from 45% to 35%, and it stayed there for almost forty years.

Thomas Robert Malthus, many years ago, also formulated a similar "irreversible" process in connection with a constantly increasing population. At the time he was writing, things probably looked desperate, but the situation did not evolve according to his predictions. The same can be said about the position of David Ricardo, regarding the prices of agricultural land, which were constantly increasing, with undesirable consequences for the distribution of created wealth. Yet later developments showed that the GNP was influenced more by other sources of wealth, than by the price of agricultural land. Marx, too, had postulated that the perpetual accumulation of capital was an "irreversible" process which he predicted to be the gravedigger of capitalism. Eventually, the increase of productivity proved him wrong.

With all these "irreversible" examples dealing with social issues, we should always keep in mind that social laws are not like the laws of physics. Regarding chaos, the ancient Greeks had reached the conclusion that one should not try to predict the future using information that is yet unknown. Thus, what can be explained about today's society is true for today only, or, in any case, only for a short time, whereas the law of gravity, for example, is valid for all time. That is how the presence of the moon orbiting around our planet helped to produce life down here (which otherwise could not have been generated in the absence of the phenomenon of tides, which provided the necessary constant motion). On the other hand, no matter how advanced our technology may get, decisions are made by humans, not by technology. What technology can do, is assist our endeavors. Or does one think that we will eventually manage to construct the perfect robot, which will absolve us from any need to think? No one knows, but judging by the current state of things, our youngsters, who are so busy with their personal phones, find no time for physical exercise. If the ancient Greeks are right in saying that a healthy mind is to be found only in a sound body, then the future, most probably, may come to an end regardless of this intelligent robot! One does not know which one will come first: the intelligent robot, or the catastrophic climate changes. An optimist, like me, will probably say that true democracy will be the first to reach the finishing line in this race.

Ulrich Beck (44) provides eight strong reasons that make the precept of universality a one-way street for humankind, when taken in the right direction, and he also demonstrates ten areas where universality can give sustainable political answers. What he does is to reinvent the wheel. All of his points are also goals, to which **truly democratic systems of government should aspire**, i.e. governments that will not derive from the actions of the bosses of multinationals, but only from the mass-involvement of citizens in daily events, at least in those countries where some democratic rule still exists. Alas, we don't see any religions doing something effective to encourage the mass-involvement of their followers in order to ensure at the same time the salvation of their souls.

What is really needed is the existence and operation of true democratic rule, especially in those nations that have a great responsibility for what is happening around the globe. Only a genuinely democratic rule can raise the level of culture in our societies, which is critically needed today, and in that respect some religions can help true democracies to arrive at their final objectives sooner. I do not expect Erdogan's Islamism to contribute much in this field, as long as all that is happening on earth is still God's work, in which case the only ones who can do the job are the respective religious leaders, who do represent God's will on earth. However, I am one of those who believe that only cultured people can run the above-mentioned corporations on a basis of ethical conduct, and while some religions can contribute to that effort, only in countries under a genuine democratic rule will their efforts have positive results.

As we have said right from the start, the model of democracy proposed in this book constitutes a means to an important end, which is the welfare of all members of a society. Assuming that this model is the appropriate one, and that some country may agree to introduce it and implement it, can we then expect it to produce the desired results?

There is a well-known saying: **one swallow does not make a summer**. Democracy can start in a country, but it must spread across every continent for it to make a difference. Also, more is required for things to start changing. We need cultured societies, which are produced only by true democratic countries, but even these latter cannot generate the former overnight. In our times, more is required for democracy to start producing the desired results. From the beginning, one major obstacle will be the international political and economic environment, which "whistles" to the tune of the current capitalist model of production. The present political system was constructed many years ago for the purpose of serving efficiently the capitalist model of production. It was formally given the name of democracy, even though we know that it serves very inadequately the democratic principles that define democracy. As a result, through years of brainwashing, just over half of the people are today addicted to and believe that the election process is a good tool for democracy. Nevertheless, this does represent most of the people around the globe, who are convinced that this system is democratic because elections are held. After all they are "free" to vote and make "their" choices of the governments they prefer.

All societies in all the Western democracies around the world are addicted to the process of election which for them is the alpha and omega of democracy. For them, democracy and elections mean the same thing. Few know better, and can, therefore, differentiate between the two. In ancient Athenian democracy this tool was not used to elect politicians, but only experts in different fields. The political body, namely their parliament, was formed by non-professional politicians. They were ordinary people who were selected by sortition and for a single term only. The body that had absolute political power in that democracy was the citizen's assembly. **This also was a tool.** It was chosen by the Athenians for the purpose of serving the axiomatic principles of democracy. This tool also did not elect politicians. This body **was** the government and its members were, on some occasions, electing special experts. **Therefore, those who invented democracy did not use elections to run their democracy.** Everybody must understand this. One should not mistake the one for other. **The tools do not define the system;** they are there to serve the system, which is defined by its axiomatic principles. Some tools, which were selected to serve "modern" democracies, have failed in their mission. Instead, they have served, and continue to serve, political systems of the oligarchic type. Nevertheless, they are being called democracies without being ones. One such tool is the election process, which today is used for everything. The other is the tradition of vocational politics, which requires renewal of the term in office, whereby collusion is produced. **The axiomatic principles of democracy are universal values; tools are not.**

Generally, the right policies come from true democratic governments, and without them one cannot expect much. These policies are more of a political and less of an economic type, even though economic policies may affect political ones. To my knowledge, the axiomatic principles of democracy, up to now, have not been served well by the tools invented and used by those in charge. The tools societies have adopted from time immemorial, judging based on the results produced, have been proven to be far from being the right ones. The policies that have been adopted and promoted by the tools invented so far, fall short of any lasting success. For these reasons, more people are seeking to find or invent different but more promising tools, which will serve better the axiomatic principles that define democracy. **In short, the tools used for serving democracy have failed and must be changed. It is as simple as that.**

The present economic status quo has been the result of a continuous struggle between capitalism and the working class, organized or not. It is a struggle entirely based on a collision course between the two, which produced wars of all kinds, and a state of hate and distrust in the relations between the two sides, culminating in the attitude of **the winner takes all.**

One should not be surprised, then, that societies have been behaving not so very differently from those at the dawn of humankind as regards people's conduct towards one another. The reason is that human nature cannot be changed. Some philosophers have stated that people's behavior cannot be any different. They even developed, based on their thesis, whole theories which condemn societies to a constant state of savage antagonism and destruction, through which "progress" is made. And, which is more offensive, they call this progress culture or civilization. According to these philosophical precepts, all the axiomatic principles of democracy appear to be just a utopia. No wonder then that all the tools proposed and used so far by the existing democracies are in line with this one precept, namely every man for himself. This social status quo cannot reflect and does not reflect cultured societies. This is where we have been now for some time, namely living in social jungles, and if we accept this, then it will truly be the fate of our societies, as the philosophers have prescribed it for us. For if we do not take the decision to make the necessary changes, things will get worse.

It is well known that the capitalist model of production does at least go hand in hand with the different religions. All religions, judging based on their manifesto voted by their parliament in Chicago, have accepted the theory of the capitalist modus operandi, though, to give them credit, not the actual practice, just a modified version. Since then, conditions have deteriorated, which means that good intentions are not enough. What is needed are the right actions that will lead to true democratic states. Yet what do we see happening in real life? On the one hand we have religions pursuing, according to their teachings, a road that leads to the salvation of their followers' souls, who must also make some sacrifices along the way in order to achieve this, and on the other hand we have the capitalist model of production pursuing the road leading to a state of "dog eats dog." This kind of situation somehow accomplishes the impossible: eat one's cake and have it too! It appears that someone ought to explain this paradox, for this coexistence is regarded as being responsible for the schizophrenic behavior of the members of all the societies concerned. And this explanation ought to come from the religious leaders, who, beyond some public ceremonies, have not provided so far, any explanation of this sinful symbiosis. **Don't religious leaders understand that their efforts to save the souls of their followers, which is, anyway, their divine mission on earth, is undermined by the works of the present capitalist model of production? Or do they believe that what is produced under the capitalist model is divine labor?**

One thing is certain: this has not been the work of a true democratic system, neither the work of God. Democracy does not pull the two forces – rich and poor – apart, and neither should religions. Democracy tries to bring these forces closer, and to develop a spirit of trust between them. For this to be achieved, the equilibrium between the two forces must be preserved unremittingly. As **Solon** said many centuries ago, **neither the poor nor the rich should be able to win an unjust case.** Democracy can work where trust exists between the different parties. Democracy can create such environments, not overnight, but in due time, and through great effort. The new type of political parties can and must play a prominent role in this interim period. One should remember that with all the proposed changes, especially in the area of the media and the funding of the political parties, economic considerations will necessarily take a back seat on this journey. Economics will continue to play a role in politics, but now the character of their involvement is entirely different. Economics will have to concern themselves exclusively with standards of success as regards the welfare of the members of society, and not with the excessive profits of capital. The areas of concern in a normally operating democracy will be **the creation of trust among the parties involved, as well as the encouragement of the creative members of society to pursue their endeavors, and thus, through their**

**inventions and competence, contribute the means for reaching the set objectives of the society in question, and within the framework of a truly free market. All working people make an important contribution to the overall effort for our survival, but thinking people and creative people are those who move the world forward, and those people should have our respect and the means to go on, in order to broaden our horizons and the spectrum of opportunities for all. These pioneers in helping move the world forward will enjoy universal respect in a true democratic system. As things are today, these pioneers, instead of respect, "enjoy" only ruthless exploitation.**

The way events are unfolding, our societies are being forced today towards dangerous dead ends against their will. These developments will lead to very explosive situations which will not be controllable. It is very urgent, therefore, for the present system of governments to undergo major reforms, which will eventually lead our societies to a system that will be under the aegis of true democracy. Otherwise, the injustices and inequalities will continue to creep in, and eventually lead to unforeseeable consequences.

The just distribution of created wealth is primarily a political issue. In our present world, under the current democracies, even political decisions are not capable of regulating the process. Thomas Piketty's (13) proposal for taxing the rich has not found open ears. One should keep in mind that our societies are just modern barbaric societies, armed with modern destructive means, and their members, alas, have but one vision: that of every man for himself. Even a true democratic government will need time to transform our modern societies to the point where they can accept the just distribution of created wealth. This issue is not economic; it is not even political under the present democracies. It is primarily cultural. Cultural, but not in the sense of beautiful architectural buildings. That is not culture, as it has been explained in a previous chapter; it is just the result of specially trained people, while culture signifies a stance on the part of the members of a society, a shared vision that focuses on the welfare of all. This should be branded deeply in our minds and we should fight for it, if we want to see the just distribution of created wealth to really take place, and an end to the mass movements of people from one country to another, as it is happening today. Thinking people in our societies, who have an appropriate vision for our cultured world, must come up with ways to reach the desired results under these new conditions.

Trust between parties can be achieved when the representatives of different interests agree upon a credible modus operandi that will benefit, as initially agreed, all parts of the cooperative effort. Human nature will certainly be pushing constantly in the direction of self-interest, and the momentum of the people involved will always be towards primitive barbarity, where the big fish eats the small fish. Some of these trends can be improved by reaching agreements from which all people involved will benefit accordingly. In addition, the more cultured the members of the parties involved are, the easier it will be for this restructuring to succeed. The framework upon which all the models will initially operate will be based on a transparent cooperation between the state and private citizens. The objective, in the long run, will be to create an operational framework based on trust and solidarity among the members of society.

Under current conditions, capital, on an international level, has more options than the people working in any enterprise. In the first instance, capital can avail itself of safe-haven countries, which provide it with many benefits regarding opportunities for higher profits. This, objectively, poses a serious constraint for working people, who have less leverage to negotiate higher incomes and other benefits. Under such circumstances, the emerging conditions also constitute a serious constraint for democracy overall. The whole situation is very difficult, especially when the issue of security enters the picture, giving some of those who control the capital second thoughts about the whole matter. **This is where a democratic government can provide all the necessary assurances to those who control the capital, through sufficient legislation that will convince them of their capital's security, of their investments being safe in the short and in the long term, provided that capital is now ready to pay its dues to society.**

The way things look today, the international economic situation is not very promising for working people, especially in smaller and poorer nations. The United Nations have not produced the required conditions either. The prospects envisaged for the future, as we have seen, are mostly under the control and supervision of multinational corporations. Some efforts by the United Nations to promote ethical conduct among the corporations have not really produced impressive results. The reason may be that countries, where the status quo of multinationals has been strengthened beyond any control, still operate under the same model of production. These conditions can only be changed (gradually, obviously) when democracies will be established in most of the countries around the globe. As one can see there is a lot of work ahead of us.

## 5.2 General Closing Remarks

The Oxford professor Paul Collier, in his book titled *The Future of Capitalism (12)*, states that he wrote this book for the people. Obviously, he has little or no hope that the present political establishment will go ahead and make use of his advice to change itself. His hope derives from the assumption that, once people have the right knowledge, they will make the right decisions when the election time comes, and will vote for pragmatist politicians who will, presumably, correct some policies which the system has in any case produced not just once, but many times.

The Harvard professor Lawrence Lessing (15), in the preface of his book, titled *They Don't Represent Us*, writes that "The system that has failed America will not change unless we "challenge it" and make it change." Reading through the various chapters one discovers that this can be accomplished by informing the people of their rights, and teaching them how the government works, so one can demand it to operate democratically.

Steven Lesky and Daniel Ziblatt (37), both Harvard professors, and authors of the book *How Democracies Die*, write in turn that "Military coups and other violent seizures of power are rare. Most countries hold regular elections. Democracies still die, but by different means." **I say, they die because of the regular elections.** They have themselves put the official seal of approval on the grave where democracies are buried.

One important conclusion that can be drawn from the above is that there is a widespread confusion, intentional or not, about what is and what is not democracy. The confusion stems from the fact that democracy is, conveniently, defined by a tool, namely the process of electing politicians, and not by the axiomatic principles of democracy, which is the right way to define democracy. The ancient Athenian democracy never used elections to select its politicians, and therefore Aristotle defines a governing system where elections are used to select politicians as an oligarchic, not a democratic, system of government.

My book has also been written for the people; for politicians are not and will not be moved by my proposed model of democracy, for this model ends the politicians' careers. However, this book differs from the others, because it offers the people new tools to fight for real changes. Other books, even though they contain very useful proposals, do not give new appropriate tools to the people to fight for real change. They leave them with the same tool that is responsible for today's mess.

Which are the new tools proposed by this book that really come to the aid of democracy?

1. A new type of political party free of any collusion or dependency on outside centers of influence. This is accomplished by selecting all the political officers of the party by sortition and for one term only. Political officers of party structures who are selected by lot must meet the requirements set for each position.

2. A new tool for electing the leader of the party, namely the Regional Assemblies, where all voters are free of any collusion and dependency towards the candidate for the leadership of the party, or towards any other center of influence, within or outside the party. The candidates for party leadership now have only one way to reach the top, and that is their competence, their overall knowledge, and their character. They will no longer be able to influence the voters by promising favors for positions in the party, or for a renewal of their term in office!

3. A similar tool as that used for the election of the candidate for party leadership, is proposed for the election of the mayoral party candidate in each region.

4. A new tool for selecting, for one term only, party candidates for parliament, and for the local councils of the local government, consisting of a procedure that entails a double sortition. The first sortition determines the specific electoral list of the party (details are mentioned in chapters 2 and 3), and the second sortition, which takes place after the elections, determines the ranking of each candidate on that list (first, second etc., to be stipulated on the basis of the percentage of votes won by the party). This procedure removes from anyone the potential to influence who gets elected and who is not. In this way, all those elected are free of any collusion or dependency to anyone. With this procedure, every region will have, for the first time, true representatives, free of any collusion and dependency, promoting the welfare of the people.

What is important to emphasize in conclusion, is that no constitutional changes are initially required in order to start the process of forming movements or parties of all ideological preferences that pronounce themselves to be lovers of democracy. These movements, which are free of collusion and dependency, will now fight for real changes to happen using as their sole platforms the parliament and the country's city councils.

As we reach the end of this book, a few words must be addressed to the proponents of the idea of the citizens' assembly. Among the most recent reforms that are being put forth for us to come closer to a true democratic government, the most prominent is the citizens' assembly, which was used in ancient Athenian democracy. This institution was itself the government at that time. All powers were vested in it. It could do anything it wanted. This institution was christened direct democracy, because all male citizens over the age of twenty could participate in it, and because in this assembly they could speak and vote on laws, approve foreign and defense policies, elect experts, convict someone who was found guilty even to death, or exile the enemies of democracy, as well as do many other things a government does. Many people today like this idea, and therefore they promote the citizens' assembly. To them, it means that the people are in power. Others, because of the increase in population numbers, regard the citizens' assembly as a utopia. As far as I am concerned, the citizens' assembly is a very bad form of government, widely susceptible to strong centers of influence, thus opening the back door to the capitalist model of production, as it works today, in order to continue business as before. In the main body of this book, I have explained how this happens. The Athenian citizens' assembly in fact turned out to be the Trojan horse that prevented democracy from growing deep roots. After all, the idea of a citizens' assembly can be enforced only through revolution, and that would be a terrifying prospect.

My proposed model on the other hand has no need of a revolution in order to be implemented. It can initiate the required reforms immediately based on what we have already. These are the political parties (scorned, of late, by many), which can be reformed, and be transformed, from being servants of the capitalist model of production into being rather a foundation which will allow true democracy to thrive. So instead of citizens' assemblies, which lead to dead ends, people should start forming new political parties, if the old ones refuse to be reformed, with the structural components proposed in this book.

It is the only path, in my opinion, through which true democracy may be revived someday. And it is the easiest of all other proposed paths.

In Antiquity, the population was not very large, nor was it scattered across vast areas. The population of the ancient Athenian city-state numbered around 170,000 people. The participants in the citizens' assembly, in addition to the political officers (who were over the age of 30 and selected by sortition), were men only, who were over the age of twenty. Even then, as has been mentioned before, participation was limited, and the synthesis of the group that could participate, was, from the point of view of social and geographical background, very poor. In that respect, the citizens' assembly could not really qualify as a form of government of direct democracy. According to reliable historical sources, a 10% level of participation was a rare upper limit. Today, when we consider 50 to 60% participation in elections as being poor, what would this 10% be? Perhaps it was because of this poor participation, that the results produced in the Athenian democracy were so remarkable. Can one imagine what chaos would have been created in those citizens' assemblies if participation in them was even just 50%? It is then time we questioned seriously the operationality of citizens' assemblies as a form of government, and sought, in a logical and not in a sentimental manner, ways of devising tools that will serve more credibly the axiomatic principles of democracy today. One also must keep in mind that collusion is free to enter the deliberations of such assemblies and spoil the whole process. It happened then, and it can happen again especially today. Nevertheless, having said that, one cannot but praise the system of government in ancient Athens, not only because of the unique results this system produced, which became the foundations of Western civilization, but also because at that time this system of government was actually a heavenly oasis compared to what other systems of government existed around the globe.

Today, we have technologies which can help us, not only to overcome some of the difficulties that were encountered by the ancient Athenians, but also to address present problems for the purpose of improving the overall result. However, no matter what technologies one may have available, if the model, and more specifically the tools, are not the right ones, the results will be very disappointing. One should keep in mind that elections, used as a means to elect members of parliament and other political officers in party structures, constitute an event of direct democracy. Nevertheless, the benefits created for the people do not match their expectation. However, this election tool could improve the situation greatly if only the members of parliament were elected for one and single term. Their dependency on party bosses of any kind or on outside centers of influence will be reduced immensely. One can then imagine what will happen to the phenomenon of collusion, which dominates all different types of political affairs today, if the composition of the electoral lists and the determination of the rankings of each candidate on the list after the election, was done using the sortition tool, a process that has been described elsewhere in this book.

One should not forget that almost half the voters don't even take the trouble to go and cast their vote, for they do not believe that anything can change. Many voters, because of the bad results produced, blame the other tool used in today's democracies, namely that of the institution of the political party, and not the tool of the election process itself. After all, this is usual practice: blaming others for every sin, rather than blaming oneself. As a result, proponents for the citizens' assembly abound, and what we end up doing is simply changing platforms by going back and forth, from **Scylla to Charybdis.** The same could be said regarding the different types of plebiscites (referendums) being held. Neither of these two forms of direct democracy has delivered satisfying results, and in some cases of plebiscites, governments totally ignored the results and did quite the opposite.

In our time, any cases of direct democracy (whether elections or plebiscites) have not provided very desirable results so far, as they did in the direct democracy of ancient Athens, even if there were exceptions even then. **It was not the direct democracy of ancient Athens that created the wonders of that period, but the use of sortition, which secured political equality among the candidates who wished to volunteer for political positions. This process kept those in political positions, namely the 500 parliamentarians, who were selected by lot for one term only, free of any dependency upon centers of influence, and it also deprived the holders of political office of the possibility of becoming professional politicians.**

Finally, the media in a truly democratic system will not be able in practice to influence events as much as they can do today, not to mention the fact that many of today's services to politicians will no longer be needed. However, the proper use of the media in a democratic country can improve many of the limitations faced by the ancient Athenians.

The question we are trying to answer is how to satisfy the basic principles of democracy. Our objective, therefore, is to prescribe the type of tools that will give the process of democracy the means by which we reach our goal, which is the welfare of all. It is worth pointing out that these measures or changes should not be followed like a religious dogma – of which we have plenty. We do not need more shackles or chains. Someone else can perhaps even come up with a more efficient and appropriate model than the one proposed here. The question is: **is there a will to put the necessary reforms into practice by applying some of the main essential tools used in ancient Athens to our political institutions, such as, for one thing, the political parties? I wish to stress once more that the importance of the proposed model for reviving democracy is that some parts of it can be implemented straight away, because they do not require any constitutional changes.**

Whatever we may think about the proposed reforms, one effect will be that with them, political decisions, and the control of their implementation through specific bodies, are now in the hands of a different kind of politician, the kind that will truly represent the interests of the people. On the other hand, the implementation of policies that have been decided by politicians in the cabinet and in parliament will be implemented by independent authorities that are managed by experts. These are now under the strict scrutiny of parliament in its new role, and they can therefore be monitored more effectively than is the case with elected politicians, who can easily brand any review of their work as a form of political persecution. This must be regarded as a great accomplishment for a governmental reform, and it does not require a vast number of constitutional changes. We can be sure that these major reforms over time will lead to others. As with any system, democracy, too, will constantly need modernization.

# References


1. Aristotle, *Constitution of the Athenians*, transl. H. Rackham, Cambridge: CUP, 1935

2. *Athinaiki Dimokratia*, Akadimia Athinon 1995, Athens Greece

3. *Aisthitiki Ton Archeon Ellinon*, Transl. Alexios Petrou, *To Bima* 2015

4. Sakelariou, M.B., I *Athinaiki Dimokratia*, Publised by the University Of Crete.

5. Yiannis Th. Giannopoulos, *Politia Ke Ethos*, Patra 1983

6. Paul Cartlege, *Democracy: A lifetime*, Oxford University Press 2018

7. Claude Mossé, *Regards Sur La Démocratie Athénienne*, Paris: Perin, 2013

8. Sinclair, R. K., *Democracy and Participation in Athens*, Cambridge: CUP, 2011

9. Ch. G. Starr, I *Gennesi Tis Athinaikis Dimokratias* Ekdosis . ardamitsa

10. Kornilios astoriadis, *I Archea EllinikiDdimikratia Kai I Simasia Tis Gia Mas Simera*, Dialexi sto Leonidio, psilon/ L , thina 1999

11. Adam Swift, *Politiki Philosophia*, Ekdosis Okto 2014

12. Collier, Paul, *The Future of Capitalism*, HarperCollins Publishers, New York

13. Piketty, Thomas, *Le Capital Au XXIe Siècle*, Paris: Le Seuil, *2013*

14. Paraskeyopoulos, M. N.

15. Lessing, Lawrence, *They Don't Represent Us*, DAY ST., an imprint of William Morrow for information, address HarperCollins Publishers, 195 Broadway, New York 10007

16. Van Reybrouck, David, *Against Elections*

17. Dowlen, Oliver, *Sorted: Civil Lotteries and The Future Of Public Participation*

18. *Apathetic about Democracy: Engaging Young Voters* Written by Mary Scott. Mary Scott is a researcher for Catch 21. Catch 21 is a charitable production company which organizes and stages shows all over the UK with the key aim of engaging those currently disengaged, especially young people, with politics.

19. United Kingdom's Election Commission of 2002, on its report: *Voter Engagement and Young People*

20. Blondel, J., Sinnot, R. and Svensson, P. (1998) *People and Parliament In The European Union*, Clarendon Press, Oxford

21. Dalton, R. (1988) *Citizen Politics: Public Opinion and Political Parties in Advanced Western Democracies*, Chatham House, Chatham, NJ

22. Lutz, J. (1991); Marginality, Major and Third Parties and Turnout in England in 1970s and 1980s: *A R-analysis and Extension*, Political Studies, Vol. 39 pp.721–6.

23. Whiteley, P., Harke, H., and Sanders, D. (2001), *Turnout*, in P. Morris (eds), Britten Votes 2001, Cambridge University Press, Cambridge.

24. Franklin, M. (1996) *Electoral Participation*, in L. LeDuc, R. Niemi and P. Norris (eds), *Comparing Democracies: Elections and Voting in Global Perspective*, Sage, Thousand Oaks, CA

25. Blais, A. (2000) *To Vote or Not to Vote? The Merits and Limits of Rational Choice Theory*, University of Pittsburgh Press, Pittsburgh, PA.

26. Market and Opinion Research International (MORI) in its 2001, (http://www.mori.com/polls

27. Carnegie Young People's Initiative, Ravi Gurumurthy

28. The British Social Attitude Survey

29. Criddle, B. (2001) 'MPs and Candidates,' in D. Butler and D. Kavanagh, *The British General Election of 2001*, Palgrave, Basingstoke

30. Huggins, R. (2001) *The Transformation of the Political Audience*, B. Axford and R. Huggins (eds), *News Media and Politics*, Sage, London

31. Dionne, E. (1991) *Why Americans Hate Politics*, Simon & Schuster, New York, NY

32. Nye, J. (1997) *Why People Don't Trust Government*, Harvard University Press, Cambridge, MA

33. Eliasoph, N. (1998) *Avoiding Politics: How Americans Produce Apathy in Everyday Life*, Cambridge University Press, Cambridge

34. International Institute for Democracy and Electoral Assistance (International IDEA), of Sweden in its 1999

35. Casper, Lynne M. and Loretta E. Bass, *Voting and Registration in the Election of November*, 996, Washington, D.C.: United States Census Bureau, Current Population Reports, p. 20–504 (July) p. 1, 1998.)

36. *French National Report* by Anne Muxel, Cecile Riou, Viviane Lehay, Fonation Nationale des Sciences Politiques (FNSP), March 2005, EUYOU-PART WP8/D15 Working paper on national survey results.

37. Levitsky, Steven and Ziblatt, Daniel, *"How Democracies Die,"* published by Crown New York.

38. Crosland, A. (2013), *The future of Socialism*, London: Constable.

39. Smith, A. (2010), *The Theory of Moral Sentiments*, London: Penguin.

40. Ansermet Francois – Pierre Magistretti, *a Ichni tis Embirias*, Panepistimiakes Ekdosis ritis, Iraklio 2016.

41. Andreas Schiehl and Tom Wohlfarth from the Denkzentrum/Democratie of Germany, www.denkzentrum-demokratie.de_

42. _Hans Kung – Klaus M. Leisinger – Josef Wieland, *Manifesto tis Pangosmias Ekonomikis Ethikis*, kdosis nidari, Athens Greece.

43. Smith, A., (2017), *The Wealth of Nations: An Inquiry Into the Nature of Causes*, New Delhi: Global Vision Publishing House.

44. Beck, Ulrich, *The Metamorphosis of the World*, Cambridge: Polity, 2016